BLACK MAGIC

LILY HART

BLACK MAGIC

HOW TO BE A BAD WITCH

PIATKUS

PIATKUS

First published in Great Britain in 2023 by Piatkus

10 9 8 7 6 5 4 3 2

A CIP catalogue record for this book is
available from the British Library.

ISBN 978-034943-880-1

Printed and bound in Great Britain by
Clays Ltd, Elcograf S.p.A.

Papers used by Piatkus are from well-managed
forests and other responsible sources.

MIX
Paper | Supporting
responsible forestry
FSC
www.fsc.org   FSC® C104740

Piatkus
An imprint of
Little, Brown Book Group
Carmelite House
50 Victoria Embankment
London EC4Y 0DZ

The authorised representative
in the EEA is
Hachette Ireland
8 Castlecourt Centre
Dublin 15, D15 XTP3, Ireland
(email: info@hbgi.ie)

An Hachette UK Company
www.hachette.co.uk

Why be good, when you can be bad?

CONTENTS

Part Three: Live deliciously – self-care
          inspired by the Seven
          Deadly Sins

Introduction:

WELCOME TO YOUR VILLAIN ERA

If you are tired of being meek, polite, apologetic and anxious, if you are fed up with peppering every email with 'No worries if not!' and 'Just checking in!', if you know that somewhere inside you is a hard knot of bubbling low-level rage that you never allow to surface – then we need to talk.

So many of us are taught from a young age that it is wrong or somehow rude to speak up for ourselves, put ourselves first, say what we need and want, or otherwise rock the boat. Our lives are geared towards people-pleasing, whether that's seeking the approval of a difficult boss, jumping through hoops for social media likes, or pretending it's really no big deal when a friend or romantic partner wrongs us.

When did we become so timid, so cautious – so *bland*?

The truth is, there is magic coursing through each one of us, but all too often we bury our powers, pushing them down and locking them deep inside. We pretend they aren't there, we try to be good, we turn our eyes away from the moon and towards our screens, and we hope that if we work hard and play nicely, we might one day get the things we dream of.

Well, it's time to shake things up a little. Because you might not realise it, but your feelings, wants and desires matter, and you deserve a life filled with delights. You are allowed to say no to the things that displease or straight-up bore you. You are allowed to take the things that you want and deserve. And you know all those big, powerful feelings inside you? Instead of trying to hide them behind filters and fake smiles, you can channel them into rituals, spells and enchantments. You can protect yourself from toxic people and fill your world with magic.

Come take a little walk with me on the darker side of life. It's time to enter your villain era . . .

❋ x ❋

PART ONE:

SOMETHING WICKED THIS WAY COMES

'A witch ought never to be frightened in the darkest forest . . . because she should be sure in her soul that the most terrifying thing in the forest was her.'
— Terry Pratchett, *Wintersmith*

Chapter I:

A BRIEF HISTORY OF WITCHES

Before we dive in and start exploring how you can embrace your own witchiness and make your life a little more magical, let's take some time to consider the history and mythology of witches. For millennia, the witch has been a maligned and feared figure, and this misplaced fear has led to the deaths of many thousands of innocent people. As we embrace witchcraft and proudly call ourselves witches, it's important to acknowledge those who have gone before us, whether they identified themselves as witches or had the label thrust upon them.

Ancient witches

Witchcraft and magic have deep roots in folklore and world history. Almost every culture throughout history has believed in – and often feared

– witches. Here, we'll be looking mainly at witch-craft traditions in the Western world, but there is a rich and varied global history of witchcraft and magic that is endlessly fascinating.

Glimpses of witchy activity, from ceremonies and spellcraft to full-blown transmutations, can be seen in ancient cultures, including those of Greece, Rome and Egypt. In ancient Egypt, powerful priests cast spells in temples as part of complex rituals, while the second-century writer Apuleius, himself accused of witchcraft, wrote a novel featuring women who worked magical spells to achieve their desires. The myths of ancient Greece are peppered with sorcerers, from the enchantress Circe, who transformed Odysseus's crew into pigs after they behaved like, well, pigs, to her niece Medea, who used her magic to help Jason on his quest for the Golden Fleece. While the witches of Greek mythology are often beautiful women and love interests, in ancient Roman literature witches are generally depicted as fearful, hid-eous creatures – such as the foul-breathed Erichtho, who had a fondness for raiding graves and raising the dead – and this more negative depiction was reflected in society's horror of witchcraft. Meanwhile, in Celtic mythology, the fearsome and powerful Morrígan, the unstoppably badass goddess of war and fate, was often presented as a witch or sorceress, while Ceridwen, a Welsh white witch, was known for brewing powerful potions.

In each tradition, the natural world played a significant role in tales of witchcraft and supernatural power, with witches said to call on the sun, the moon, the sea and the earth to add potency to their spells, as well as taking on familiars in the form of animals or using plants and herbs in their simmering cauldrons. The changing seasons also played an important role in legends around magic, and Celtic traditions included celebrations that are familiar to many witches today, including solstices and other seasonal festivals such as Samhain, Imbolc, Beltane and Lughnasa. Over time, these practices grew into what became known as Paganism, incorporating various folkloric beliefs, along with spells and rituals.

The witch hunts

Throughout history, people who don't fit in have been labelled as witches and ostracised. Their sins might include daring to live alone, refusing to follow societal conventions, or having the gall to be intellectually adept or sexually liberated. From Anne Boleyn to Joan of Arc, people who don't toe the line have been called witches. (Just a note here that although we tend to associate witchcraft with women, it is not gender-specific – anyone can be a witch. The majority of those executed during the witch hunts were women, and the hunts themselves were largely perpetrated by powerful men – *quelle surprise* – but people of all genders have been persecuted for witchcraft.)

As we've seen, witches and magic have always featured in mythology and cultural histories, but it was with the growth of the Christian Church that there came a real fear of 'witchcraft' and those thought to practise it. By the early Middle Ages, the Church considered attempts to use magic as demonic and evil, describing them as '*maleficium*', meaning harmful. The fear continued to brew like a particularly potent potion, and by the 1300s, it had reached new levels, with Pope John XXII excommunicating those suspected of working ceremonial magic, including some people within his own court. The following century, Pope Innocent VIII sent out his inquisitors, and the practice of actively hunting for witches began.

In 1486, German Catholic priest Heinrich Kramer wrote the *Malleus Maleficarum*, a rambling and often muddled tract about witches and their supposed practices. He insisted that 'a greater number of witches is found in the fragile feminine sex than among men', and that these 'fragile' creatures spent a great deal of time having sex with demons and flying (presumably on their way to have sex with more demons). The text became an essential resource for witch hunters over the following centuries.

Most of the people who were accused of being witches were simple country folk who still used skills and remedies that had been handed down through generations. Suddenly, brewing up a poultice with some herbs to soothe an injury, or marking a particular point in the calendar with a traditional celebration, became regarded with suspicion. Some people used the witch hunts as a way to get revenge on neighbours whom they disliked or distrusted. If someone pissed you off at church on Sunday, you could accuse them of witchcraft on Monday and rapidly unravel their life. When crops failed or illness struck, people tended to turn to witchery as the cause rather than considering the possibility that such events might be due to poor weather or the spread of a virus.

As the panic grew, there were widespread witch hunts across Europe and later, the New World and the colonies. Those accused were kept in horrific conditions, locked in filthy cells and often starved. They were stripped naked in search of 'devil's marks' and pricked with pins to see if they bled. Failure to bleed meant witchery was afoot, but historians have examined tools used by witchfinders and found retractable needles and other trickery to ensure the result the witchfinder wanted.

Some witch hunters employed the infamous practice of 'ducking', where an accused witch was bound and thrown into water. If they floated, they were considered to be working with the devil and guilty of witchcraft. If they drowned, they were innocent (but dead).

The use of torture was common, and the accused were often forced to confess through the most vicious of methods.

From the brutal trial of Margaret Aitken in Scotland in the late 1500s, which saw her tortured not only into confessing but also accusing many others, to the infamous Salem witch trials of the 1690s, the persecution and execution of witches shaped our history and changed our culture. From 1400 onwards, it's believed 40–60,000 people were put to death for witchcraft during these trials, with the peak between 1560 and 1640. The last person to be executed for witchcraft in Europe was in 1782 in Poland. When you consider how many people were brutally tortured, abused and executed during these horrific trials, it becomes particularly galling when modern-day public figures (usually powerful men) describe themselves as victims of a 'witch hunt' when usually what's really happening is they are being criticised or made to face the consequences of their own actions. After being impeached, ex-US President Donald Trump famously described himself as the victim of 'the greatest witch hunt in the history of our country'.

Somebody buy that man a history book.

Witches today

As the panic died down, many people stopped believing in witches, and mythology and fairy tales took over, slowly building the image of the witch that many of us grew up with – the old lady in the woods, brewing potions in a simmering pot or cackling as she casts wicked spells.

However, in quiet corners, old traditions were being revived, and new traditions were being born. In the twentieth century, groups of witches began to grow in number and confidence, and in 1954, Gerald Gardner published *Witchcraft Today*, catapulting witchcraft – and a new religion, Wicca – into the spotlight.

These days, witchcraft is often understood as a practice. This practice may be part of a religion, such as Wicca or Paganism, but it doesn't have to be. Some witches like to work as part of a coven, gathering to carry out rituals or celebrate sabbats. Some prefer to do their own thing and practise as solitary witches. Witches might follow different traditions or develop their own. With our world more connected than ever before, witches are meeting each other online, sharing spells and rituals and growing in number and power. From the online mass hexing of Donald Trump to the rise of WitchTok, one thing is clear.

We're still here.

Chapter 2:

REFRAMING DARK MAGIC

We've all heard of 'good' witches and 'wicked' witches, of white magic and black magic. But what do these terms mean?

Over the years, the idea of black magic has come to be associated with things like making pacts with demons, worshipping the devil or attempting to raise the dead. If that's your bag, no shade, but it's not what I'm talking about here.

White magic is traditionally viewed as magic performed for selfless or benevolent reasons, usually to heal or help other people. Generally, magic is considered to be black or dark magic if it's performed for selfish or malicious reasons, particularly if the intention is to influence another person's free will or harm them. It's easy enough to understand how black magic came to be viewed in a negative light, and we all remember childhood fairy tales of wicked witches spinning dastardly spells and poisoning apples, while good witches enjoyed much more wholesome activities like baking and gardening.

But nobody can be all sweetness and light all the time, and sometimes, well . . . it's fun to be just a little bit bad.

In this book, we're going to be looking at things a little differently, by embracing the slightly darker side of ourselves, exploring the way we really feel and looking at the things we really want, instead of denying our 'uglier' feelings or trying to pretend to be something we're not.

Rage, frustration, bitterness, jealousy: keeping these feelings inside can make them harden and turn even more sour – and then one day you do something like throw your phone in a fountain or tell your boss to get fucked.

Of course, telling someone where to go certainly isn't a bad thing (and bad witches feel able to speak up for themselves when the time calls for it), but what if we expressed ourselves when we needed to so that we were more in control of it, rather than letting things build up until we can't bear it any more? What if we channelled these powerful feelings into a kind of magic that works for us?

What if we put ourselves first?

A person who truly knows themself isn't afraid to reveal their more shadowy side. They know the dark and the light in each of us combine to make us stronger, more powerful, and a lot more badass.

Is it really so bad to be bad?

Let's take a closer look at some of the 'wicked witches' from fairy tales, mythology and folklore. Maybe they were on to something.

Ursula, *The Little Mermaid*

Quite apart from the fact she wore a red lip like nobody's business, there's a lot to admire about the cephalopod everyone loves to hate. For one thing, Ursula was zero bullshit. She didn't *trick* anyone. She gave Ariel a clearly worded contract explaining exactly what would happen when they worked together, and then delivered exactly what she promised to deliver. She might have had her own agenda, but who doesn't? She was a boss babe running a business, and doing it with style.

Maleficent

Another devotee of crimson lipstick, Maleficent is bold, powerful and unafraid to stand up for herself. Admittedly, cursing an innocent child was a lot, but it wouldn't have happened if other people hadn't treated Maleficent so cruelly in the first place. She was perfectly happy living a peaceful life on the Moors until power-hungry men started causing trouble, stealing her wings and trying to take over her home. What's a gal to do? You mess with the bull, you get the horns.

Baba Yaga

If we dive a little deeper into folklore, we meet Baba Yaga, a witch from Slavic folklore often described as a terrifying hag (rude) who flies around in a mortar (as in pestle and mortar) and lives in a hut that stands on, I shit you not, chicken legs. This means her home can turn to face whichever direction she wishes, so not only is she a powerful witch, but she's also an architectural genius. In one of the most famous Baba Yaga stories, she takes in a young girl who has been sent out on an errand in the dangerous woods by her evil stepmother. Baba Yaga gives the girl a series of challenging tasks to perform; her reward for completing them is that Baba Yaga *doesn't* eat her (yep, a lot of her bad rap comes from the whole 'eating children' thing). But by the end of the story, Baba Yaga's tasks have actually taught the girl some valuable lessons about independence and rejecting subservience, and she is able to face her fears and gain her freedom. Baba Yaga is self-sufficient, wildly independent and full of inner strength. And she's not afraid of a few wrinkles.

Lilith

Lilith isn't technically a witch (she's most often presented as a demon), but I think she deserves a mention here. She is a dual-faceted being, presented as both a divine mother and a seductress who leads men astray. Said to have been Adam's first wife, she left him after a bitter argument during which she refused to be obedient or submissive to him, claiming they were created equal (they were both made from the earth at the same time, while Eve was later made from Adam's rib). Some versions of the legend say they fell out because he didn't want her to go on top but, whatever the reason, she left him and went on to live her best life free of his controlling ways. Lilith is presented as a cruel seductress and sometimes even a vile fiend, but really she just didn't want to put up with any bullshit from a dude – and I think we can all get on board with that.

As these wicked women show, allowing yourself to dabble in the darker side of life can help you improve your confidence, get better at setting boundaries, and put together a clearer idea of how you want your life to look. It can help you feel stronger and more in control, to name and reach for the things you really want, and make everything a little bit more delicious along the way.

A few ground rules

OK, rules don't exactly fit in with the whole rebellious vibe we've got going on here, but we need to be clear about what this book is and what it isn't. We are not summoning malevolent spirits, turning men into pigs (sorry, Circe) or poisoning any apples.

What we are doing is being bold, unashamed and gloriously selfish. We're embracing the dark and decadent side of life, because it turns out that indulging in a little black magic offers a surprising number of opportunities for truly therapeutic and powerful self-care rituals – and we deserve everything they have to offer. We're luxuriating in the things we're 'supposed' to feel bad about, and we're carving out our own space to be the witches we always wanted to be.

The rule of three

The rule of three is essentially the idea that whatever you send out into the universe, it will return to you threefold. Like karma, but in triplicate. Not all practitioners believe in it, but it's worth bearing in mind. This rule is why many people are wary of the darker side of magic; the idea of hexing someone only to have that energy return to you threefold isn't exactly appealing.

You may be wondering how this is going to fit in with the act of embracing our darker and more shadowy sides. If you practise with awareness and purpose, it's entirely possible to take bold and self-interested steps without upsetting the balance. Instead of sending new negative energy out into the universe, we'll be looking at deflecting the negative energy of others and sending it back to them, as well as practising spells and rituals to help us rise above those tedious beings who aren't worthy of our time and effort.

Do no harm

Tying in with the rule of three is the maxim 'Do no harm'. It's often heard as part of the Wiccan Rede (which translates as the 'witches' counsel', a moral code for witchy behaviour): 'And it harm none, do what ye will.'

In other words, you can do as you like, as long as you don't harm others.

We'll be taking a similar approach in this book, but with an important caveat: *Do no harm, but take no shit.*

We're not seeking to actively hurt anyone, but we're not turning the other cheek either. If people wrong you, it's OK to take steps to protect yourself and keep them from doing it again.

Before you carry out any ritual or spell, think carefully about your reasons and intentions. Consider the old adage 'be careful what you wish for', and reflect on the potential consequences of your actions. Just like you wouldn't run with scissors or let loose an arrow without checking that you're aiming at the right target (and that you really do want to fire it), intention is everything.

We're not fucking about here. We are reclaiming our own power, pushing back at people who harm us, and maybe indulging in a little mischief along the way.

A note on the dark feminine

As we've seen, the traditional idea of the witch is usually an old woman (hi again, Baba Yaga!), and historically those persecuted as witches were overwhelmingly female (although, as I said, many men were also victims of witch hunts).

However, anyone can be a witch, regardless of their gender identity. Sometimes in this book I'll talk about harnessing your dark feminine energy, but I want to be clear that you don't have to identify as female in order to have access to that energy. Each of us has both masculine and feminine energy in different amounts – the ebb and flow of these energies in each person is part of what makes us magical beings. But in a patriarchal society that values traditionally masculine attributes overall, and only rewards certain feminine attributes (while seeking to demonise or control others), each of us can dig deep within and unlock dizzying and delicious powers by channelling our darker feminine energy.

This energy is sexual, sensual, mysterious and wild. It is creative, strong yet flexible, hard to define and impossible to resist.

MAIDEN, MOTHER, CRONE

Speaking of feminine energy, some of the most potent can be found in the Triple Moon Goddess, who has three aspects – the Maiden, the Mother and the Crone – said to represent the different stages of a woman's life.

✳ Maiden – The Maiden represents beauty, enchantment, new beginnings, excitement and potential. She is youthful, innocent and forward-focused. She is associated with the waxing moon and springtime.

✳ Mother – The Mother presents fertility, growth, creation and nurturing. You don't have to have (or even like) children to identify with this archetype; you can birth a creative work or extend loving care to others around you. The Mother is calm, present and grounded. She is associated with the full moon and summer.

✳ Crone – The Crone is often misunderstood as a wicked old hag, particularly with our society's fears around ageing and death. But in truth, she personifies wisdom and a rich life, well lived. We have much to learn from her and can look forward to our own Crone years. The Crone also teaches us to slow down, rest and reflect. She is associated with the waning moon and winter.

Now that we've explored what dark magic is going to mean to us in this book, it's time to get started.

No more apologising, and no more 'No worries if not!' Take up space, light some candles, and embrace your bad witchy self.

PART TWO:

COME PLAY IN THE DARK

'Relax, it's only magic . . .'

– The Craft

Chapter 3:

BASIC WITCH

Before we start exploring spellwork and rituals, let's look at some of the basic materials and ingredients you might need, and a few other things you may want to consider.

Setting up your altar

A witch's altar is deeply personal, and the way an altar is set out will vary greatly from witch to witch. Essentially, this is a space devoted to your practice. It works as a focal point for your energy and intentions.

An altar is usually a small table or a shelf, or even a mantelpiece. If you travel a lot, you might find you prefer to create a portable altar that can fit into a box or be wrapped into a bundle and come with you on your adventures. The important thing is to respect your altar and use it only for your practice. This is not a space to let dirty dishes pile up, nor is it somewhere to set down your Pot Noodle after a night out. It is for witching, and witching only.

Cover your altar with an altar cloth – this can be anything from a silk scarf to a piece of fabric. Choose a design that feels right to you, that feels luxurious and sensual and beautiful.

What you'll keep on your altar will vary, but here are a few things to consider:

* crystals (see page 33).
* candles (see page 36).
* items from the natural world, like leaves, herbs, flowers, stones or seashells
* a pentacle – a five-pointed star. Often misunderstood as a satanic symbol, the pentacle actually represents the elements: earth, water, fire, air and spirit. It's a symbol of protection. When inverted, it takes on satanic associations.
* an athame – this is a ceremonial knife, most often used for casting circles. You don't need one to cast a circle (see page 42), but it feels awesome and looks extra as hell.

✷ a cauldron – this can be useful for burning things or making potions, but a metal/fireproof bowl will also serve your purposes.

Your Book of Shadows

A Book of Shadows was first used by Gerald Gardner, the founder of Wicca. It's a book where you can keep a record of the spells you've performed and their outcomes, and you can also note down any adjustments you make, like using different herbs or trying the spell during a different moon phase. I've shared some basic spells in this book, but I've also tried to give you lots of correspondences so, as you grow in confidence, you can begin to build your own. (In witchcraft, 'correspondences' are the meanings or particular powers associated with an ingredient or element of a spell or ritual. As you become familiar with correspondences, you can pick out particular crystals, herbs, colours and so on that will *correspond* (geddit?) with the outcome you want to achieve.)

Your Book of Shadows can be anything from an exquisitely bound journal to an old exercise book – but in the interest of embracing your inner beautiful bad witch, I suggest you go for something a little more on the decadent side.

Herbs and plants

Many spells and rituals harness the innate natural power of herbs and plants. It's something that is deeply rooted in human nature (forgive the pun). Most of us can remember making 'potions' as children in the garden, gathering petals, fallen leaves, handfuls of grass, and mixing them together in a puddle.

Turns out, not much has changed.

Herbs can be used in a number of ways. They may be used to 'dress' a candle before performing a spell or ritual (see page 38 – if you do this, just be a bit sensible about arranging your chosen flora in a way that isn't going to be a fire hazard). They can be tied into bundles and allowed to dry out, at which point you can either keep them or burn them as part of a spell. They may be combined with other elements for things like jar spells. And one of my favourite ways to use them is in ritual baths (see page 32).

Here is a selection of some of the more common herbs and plants and the kind of spellwork they can be used for.

apple – love
basil – protection, business success and wealth
black pepper – protection
caraway – passion, attracting a lover
chamomile – removing negative energy, healing, calm
chilli – healing, protection, speeding up a charm
cinnamon – cleansing, prosperity, success
clove – protection, banishing negativity
coriander – peace
cumin – protection, love, security
dandelion – communication
eucalyptus – healing
fennel seeds – money
ginger – success, love, money
lavender – calm, clarity, sleep, healing, love
mint – communication, persuasion
nutmeg – clarity, luck
rosemary – cleansing
rose petals – beauty, self-esteem, love, luck
sage – healing, purifying
thyme – protection
vanilla – love, sensuality

HERBAL BATHS

Herbal baths can be a great way to soak up the energy of your chosen herb or plant. Before you begin, check the herbs you're using are not toxic and that you don't have any allergies to them. You can either place your herbs in a muslin cloth, then tie it closed and add it to the bath (like a teabag in a truly massive cuppa), or you can just scatter them straight into the water – it feels gloriously witchy to lie in a steaming bath by candlelight surrounded by floating leaves and flowers. Think of it as chilling out in a massive cauldron (though you may want to scoop them up before you pull out the plug, or use a drain protector, otherwise you could end up with an expensive bill from your plumber). If you don't have a bath, tie your chosen herbs into a bundle and hang them near the shower head so the steam releases their fragrance, or make use of a basin and treat your tootsies to a footbath.

You might also like to add essential oils to your bath but, again, always check for allergies and skin safety – and never apply essential oils directly to the skin. If you want to use them in massage, you should always use a carrier oil.

Crystals

Crystals are a vital and beautiful part of a witch's arsenal. These ancient stones, formed deep in the earth, are full of deeply powerful energy, and they're also stunning to look at. Different crystals have different properties that can make them hugely impactful in your spellwork.

Here are some of the most common crystals and what they can be used for:

agate – worldly success
amethyst – calm, stress relief, rest
black tourmaline – protection
bloodstone – eloquence, money
citrine – wealth, prosperity, boldness, courage, victory over rivals
emerald – love, positivity, protection against deceit
fluorite* – focus, boosting creativity
granite – confidence, success, employment
haematite* – absorbs negativity, grounding
jade – protection
malachite* – enhancing social standing, prosperity
marble* – improving finances and social standing

obsidian* – achievement, protection,
  encouraging boldness
rose quartz – romantic love, family, self-love,
  self-esteem, home safety
serpentine* – attracting respect, intellectual
  power, protection from jealousy
tiger's eye – money, success, defeating
  opponents
topaz – overcoming envy
turquoise* – protection, health, wealth

CRYSTAL SAFETY

Some witches like to use crystals in their bathing rituals, or even add a piece of crystal to their water bottle. If you want to do this, carefully check whether the crystal you want to use contains any toxins that might be released into the water, and avoid any that may be unsafe. You should also check whether the crystal is porous, as this could make it vulnerable to water damage.

Cleansing crystals

Because crystals absorb energy as well as radiating it, try to cleanse them periodically, especially when you first get them. The most common way to cleanse a crystal is to leave it to soak in a bowl of saltwater overnight. (If you have access to the sea, you can wash the crystal in the sea instead.) The next day, rinse the crystal under clean running water, focusing on any negative energy being released from the stone. However, if the crystal or stone you are using is porous or 'soft' (with a rating below 6 on the Mohs hardness scale), soaking it in water, particularly saltwater, can damage it. These crystals have been marked with an * in the list on pages 33–34. To cleanse these, you can either briefly hold them under running water while focusing your energy on cleansing, or gently dab each one with a cloth lightly soaked in moon water (see page 40).

Once your crystal is cleansed, it's ready to charge.

Charging crystals

Simply set the crystal on a windowsill overnight, or somewhere safe outside where it can be bathed in the light of the moon and soak up her lunar energy. Some people like to charge their crystals in sunlight, too – I've always been more of a moon person, but do what feels right to you.

Setting intention

If you have a very particular use in mind for the crystal, once it has been charged, you can spend some time holding the stone in your hand with your eyes closed and focusing your mind on your intention. Feel the energy flow down through you into the crystal. If you like, repeat your intention aloud three times.

Candles

Let's be honest, candles are just a *vibe*, aren't they? Lighting a nice candle for ambience and glow can romanticise even the bleakest of tasks – and they're actually also very useful in terms of magic. Lots of spells and rituals make use of candles. They're a wonderful tool for concentrating your energy, and of course they literally provide you with the element of fire. Keep candles on your altar and always have a stash ready for whenever you need them.

Candle colours

When choosing a candle, select one in a colour that suits your intention.

Note: These colours don't just apply to candles: use them as a guide in general, whether you're choosing an altar cloth or deciding what to wear on a hot date.

white – purity, truth, new beginnings
black – protection, prevention, binding, repelling
   negativity
violet – wisdom
blue – calm, healing, wisdom, communication
green – abundance, monetary success, luck
yellow – creativity
orange – happiness, strength, vitality
red – love, passion, danger, career goals
pink – friendship, compassion
brown – stability
copper – money, achieving goals, professional
   growth

The flame

Some witches pay very close attention to the behaviour of the flame when they're using a

candle in a spell, and there are many interpret-
ations of what various types of flame might mean.
As a general guide, a strong, steady flame indi-
cates you have a powerful intention; a weak flame
suggests your intention is weak (so perhaps it's
worth thinking about whether you really want to
do the spell); and a dancing flame suggests that
either your energy is erratic (perhaps you aren't
focused enough) or that someone (or something)
is pushing back. Consider whether you want to
proceed.

It's worth noting that all of the above flame behaviour can also be impacted by candle/wick quality,
which is rather less exciting.

Finally – with apologies for stating the obvious –
don't leave a burning flame unattended. We're
here to tear down the system, not burn down your
house.

Dressing a candle

Some spells and rituals invite you to 'dress' your
candle(s). This doesn't mean dressing it up in a
fetching little outfit; it simply means anointing
the candle with a few drops of essential oil or
scattering some herbs or ground spices over it to

imbue it with the relevant energies. Oils can be dripped down the length of the candle, but let the oils dry before lighting. Herbs and ground spices should be scattered around the base, away from the wick. If you like, you can rub the candle with a carrier oil to help the herbs or spices stick.

The moon

The moon is deeply important to witches: her mysterious, ethereal glow oversees many of our rituals and spells, and her constant waxing and waning remind us of the ever-changing nature of life. She also controls the ebb and flow of the tides, an excellent example of the push and pull of her power.

Moon phases

This power is so impressive that the moon's phases can have a significant impact on the effectiveness of certain spells, so if you can, try to carry out these spells and rituals at the appropriate time in her cycle. This won't always be possible – if you gotta spell, you gotta spell – but it's worth doing if you can. The phases are:

new moon – setting intentions, making fresh
   starts
waxing crescent – attracting what you want,
   such as money/work
first quarter – energising, decision making,
   attracting love and luck
waxing gibbous – attracting success, taking time
   to pause and reflect
full moon – manifesting, casting love spells,
   clearing obstacles
waning gibbous – letting go of guilt/regret,
   embracing self-knowledge, cleansing, casting
   protection spells
last quarter – getting rid of toxic things,
   embracing healing and abundance
waning crescent – taking time to rest and
   recharge, practising forgiveness
   (including forgiving yourself), expressing
   gratitude

Moon water

Because of the moon's close links to water, her
gentle glow can be used to charge water with her
impressive energies. Simply set out a bowl of
water somewhere it can bathe in moonlight overnight, then use it in any spell where water is
required. Depending on the moon phase and your

intention, you can charge your water with different energies, adding an extra hit of power to your spellwork.

DAYS OF THE WEEK

Different days of the week are said to have different energies so, as with the moon phases, you might choose to perform your spellwork or ritual on a day that aligns with your intentions. You don't have to do this, but it can add another layer of power. It's also worth bearing these associations in mind when you're planning your life outside the circle – Friday is clearly a great day for a first date, while Thursday could be the perfect time to schedule a job interview.

Monday – intuition, wisdom
Tuesday – strength, protection, success
Wednesday – communication
Thursday – prosperity, luck
Friday – love, beauty, seduction
Saturday – banishing negativity, cleansing
Sunday – health, joy, ambition

Using rhyme

You'll notice that the spells I've shared in this book usually make use of rhyming incantations. Using rhymes in your spells is a personal choice. I find it helps me remember what I want to say, and it also has a sense of just being a bit more *magical*, as if the rhymes are somehow concentrating the power of the spell. That said, some witches don't like to use rhyme, or even find the whole idea a bit cringe. You do you – the incantations are a suggestion, and you can reword them as you see fit. You also don't have to say them aloud if you aren't comfortable doing so – saying them under your breath is fine, but if you don't feel comfortable giving voice to them at all, I'd ask yourself if you really are sure of your intentions and whether you truly want to cast the spell.

Drawing a circle

Before you carry out a spell, you should cast a protective circle around you. The idea here is that you are creating a barrier around yourself, a safe space from which to practise and where your energy can be focused. Casting a circle is particularly important if you feel in need of protection.

There are several ways you can draw a circle. Choose whichever feels right to you – or, as your witchy intuition grows, create your own.

Salt circle

Salt is powerful stuff – not only does it make food taste freakin' delicious, it's also an important mineral in the witching world, with strong protective qualities (and it's used in cleansing, banishing and binding spells). Casting a salt circle is very literal. Simply take a handful of salt and sprinkle it clockwise in a circle around you and your altar, ensuring everything you need for your spell is within the circle with you. As you cast the circle, imagine a powerful barrier rising up around you, keeping you safe and concentrating your powers.

Energy circle

This is the simplest method. Simply use your hand (or an athame, if you have one – not essential, but it looks badass) to cast a circle around you, moving in a clockwise direction and visualising the barrier as above.

Elemental circle

If you have more time or just feel kind of extra, try casting an elemental circle. You'll need a compass so you can identify which direction is north, east, south or west. Each compass direction is associated with an element, so place an item symbolising that element in the appropriate place, with you in the middle, forming a powerful circle around you. Some witches 'call' on the elements as they go, saying something like, 'I call on the guardians of the east, element of air; watch over my circle this night.'

Begin with east and work your way around in a clockwise direction:

east – linked with the element of air; can be
   symbolised by incense, feathers, bells;
   associated with inspiration, freedom
south – linked with the element of fire; can be
   symbolised by a candle; associated with
   protection, cleansing
west – linked with the element of water; can be
   symbolised by a cup of water or wine, or a

seashell; associated with cleansing, revitalising

north – linked with the element of earth; can be symbolised by salt, metal, a small handful of soil or a plant; associated with recovery, healing

Closing a circle

Close the circle when you finish by 'undrawing it' anticlockwise, or simply creating a break in the salt (or imagined) line. If you have chosen an elemental circle, dismantle it in an anticlockwise direction, starting with north, giving thanks to each element as you do so.

FINISHING A SPELL

Remember to finish your spells. A lot of witches say something like 'so mote it be', or 'my spell is cast', but you can choose your own finishing phrase. Remember to close the circle (see above) and thank the elements and universe.

Finding your tribe: the power of a coven

If you're a 'does not play well with others' kinda person, you may well prefer to practise alone as a solitary witch, but if you're interested in witching in company, consider seeking out a coven. A coven is simply a group of witches who gather together to work magic and perform rituals, but they may also meet on significant occasions to mark special dates or festivals. Having a coven means you have witches around you with whom you can share spells, insights and maybe a spiced margarita or three. Covens can vary in size and style, from small informal gatherings of just a few to larger groups. Some have recognised leaders, while others simply operate as a collective.

If you're interested in joining an established coven, the internet and social media can be valuable tools for helping you research any suitable groups near you, with many witches using online networks to connect with fellow occultists. You could also consider visiting your local occult or magic shop to see if they can point you in the direction of a coven, or try attending a witchcraft festival or magical meet-up to see who's around. Think about the kind of magic you want to practise and the sort of support and structure you think would work for you, then get in touch with the witches who run the coven that most appeals to you and ask them to tell you more. Many covens hold regular full-moon gatherings or sabbats, so you might be able to go along to join them for one event to see if it's a good fit. Before you attend, ask the organiser for some guidance about what to expect, whether you need to bring anything and what to wear, as some covens enjoy the ceremony and drama of wearing robes, and others even take part in the occasional skyclad (i.e. naked) ritual. A coven should always be a safe space and nobody should ever make you do anything you don't feel comfortable with, but knowing what kind of thing to expect will help you go into your first coven experience feeling confident and excited rather than apprehensive.

If you prefer the idea of putting together your own coven, reach out to some like-minded witchy pals or seek out connections online (exercising

the usual caution you'd use when meeting somebody in person for the first time – a salt circle
can't protect you if you're inviting someone into
it, after all).

There are no real rules for how big a coven
should be (and if there were, let's be honest, a
bad witch like you would probably ignore
them). Some people think a coven should be
made up of thirteen, while others favour the
elemental approach of *The Craft* and think
four is the ideal. The weird sisters of *Macbeth*
did their witching as a triad. Think about
what feels right to you and go with it. All that
matters is that you share similar goals and
values, and delight in each other's energy. A
coven is, above all else, about friendship,
connection and support.

Working with a coven can allow you to pool
your collective power and enjoy the thrill that
comes with performing a ritual or casting a
spell with your fellow witches. Plus, it's
always nice to have someone to dance around
the fire with.

✳

Now that we've covered these basics, it's time to lower the lights and dive in to embracing the bad witch you've always wanted to be.

With circle drawn
and candles lit
do no harm
but take no shit

Chapter 4:

MAIN CHARACTER ENERGY

As you begin your witchy journey towards glorious and unashamed self-love and general deliciousness, it's time to spend a while paying attention to yourself and your space.

It's easy to get sucked into other people's lives and dramas, but it's time to establish some firm boundaries and learn how to prioritise yourself. This is a bold thing to do, and it can be challenging for the people around you, especially if they are used to you being a bit of a pushover or if they expect you to be at their beck and call. They might not react well to it at first – but they're going to need to get used to it. Things are changing around here.

You are the main character in your story. You are coming into your own power and learning to love every luxurious moment of it.

Stop apologising, stop worrying about what other people think, and stop trying to please everyone else. Your pleasure comes first. It's about damn time to start living.

SELF-ACTUALISATION RITUAL

This is a ritual rather than a spell, and it's about spending time focusing on yourself, drawing on cosmic energy to truly see yourself as the beautiful, powerful soul that you are. We are conditioned by society and the media to always think we are less-than – that we're not beautiful enough, not thin enough, not curvy enough, not clever enough, not funny enough, not strong enough, not rich enough. Although there's nothing wrong with wanting more than you have (and we'll definitely be doing work to attract the things we desire later in this book), it's important to know the difference between what you want and what you think you should want. And understanding that begins with understanding yourself.

This sounds like a simple ritual, but it can actually be very challenging. We are used to looking at ourselves and others with scrutiny and judgement, but here, we look initially with an almost scientific disinterest, and then gradually with increasing love and admiration. For maximum impact, I

*recommend doing this without any make-up on –
as much as I adore my winged eyeliner, here, we're
moving towards seeing ourselves in all our unpol-
ished, wild glory. If that feels like too much to
begin with, don't worry, you can move at your own
pace.*

*It can be an emotional experience, but you got
this.*

WHAT YOU'LL NEED

a violet or purple candle
a mirror
your beautiful self

WHEN TO DO IT

You can do this any time, but try it on a Monday,
Tuesday or Sunday, or during a new moon phase
for extra impact.

WHAT TO DO

Light your candle in a safe space and take a few
deep, grounding breaths. Then sit comfortably in
front of your mirror and gaze softly at your reflection. Try to switch off those parts of your brain
that immediately begin to pick at what you can

see – *oh shit, I haven't plucked my eyebrows; damn, that's a new frown line; hmm, zit incoming* – and just *look.* Look at the flecks of colour in your eyes; look at the surface of your skin; look at the shape of your lips and the curve of your eyelashes. And – dispassionately – look at any scars or marks that you have, in the past, deemed to be imperfections. See them as they truly are: the signs of what you have survived, what you have achieved, and the deep well of strength at the very core of you.

Now, focusing your energy, begin to send feelings of love and admiration towards the person staring back at you. Notice their features; imagine the way their eyes light up when they smile. Look at their mouth, set with determination and power. Soak in their calm, steady gaze. Value and appreciate every strand of hair, every pore. Consider the dizzying network of blood vessels and veins coursing beneath their skin. Visualise that strong, beautiful heart, beating tirelessly and proudly.

Look at the wild, beautiful, enigmatic witch in the mirror.

That's you.

Spend as long as you need in communion with yourself and your dark feminine energy (see page 21). When you're ready, blow out the candle, and try to carry this new self-knowledge with you.

If you have a full-length mirror, try this standing naked in front of it, taking in your entire body. Embrace and adore every dimple, every curve, every bone, every stretch mark, the smooth parts and the not-so-smooth parts. Caress your battle scars and see yourself as the warrior witch you truly are.

Developing a mantra and creating your own sigil

Developing a mantra might not appeal to you – it can have a certain 'That Girl' (see page 123), gratitude-journal kinda vibe – but having a small, grounding and empowering phrase to repeat to yourself can be a wonderful thing.

Take some time to think about what you would like your mantra to be. You don't have to keep the same one forever, of course, and you can have more than one.

You might choose something like:

I am a bold, bad, beautiful witch
I am not afraid to dance with my shadow side
I am full of deep, dark power

Creating a sigil

One of the things that can be off-putting about a mantra is the idea that you're then going to have to write it out in cursive and hang it on your wall, à la 'Live, Laugh, Love', or post it on Instagram superimposed over a generic sunset picture (bonus points if there's a silhouette of a slim woman practising yoga in the picture too). Yawn.

Witches don't need to do that shit. Witches get to make *sigils*.

You may have seen sigils before: beautiful and mysterious-looking symbols that look almost like words or letters, but at the same time have an unfamiliar, almost otherworldly feel. Here's how to make your own.

Write out your chosen mantra or phrase, for example:

I am full of deep, dark power

Now drop any vowels, along with any repeated letters.

mfldprkpw

Now take some time and play around with the letters, arranging them into a pattern or shape. You can layer them one on top of the other, for example using the curves of the 'm' to create the 'p', 'd' and 'r', as I have here.

If you're having trouble seeing where each of the letters are, here is the sigil 'expanded'.

You can play around with the size and formation of each letter until you have a shape that's pleasing. It probably won't look anything like your original phrase; it might not even look much like it's made of letters at all. The power is locked into it with your intention. You can use this sigil whenever you want to channel its energy.

And not a smug silhouette in sight.

BECOMING 'THAT WITCH' – EMBRACING YOUR OWN WITCHY STYLE

It's by no means a requirement, but many people are drawn to the witchier side of life by the aesthetics as well as the spiritual aspects – and that's OK. We're all about beauty and physicality here. Embrace your inner Wednesday or Elvira – or, if colour is more your thing, refer to the colour guide on page 37 to help you express yourself in a rainbow of powerful shades.

It might sound silly, but wearing things like long flowing skirts or dresses, flared sleeves, darker colours and jewel tones can help you get more into the mindset of being a badass witch. Play around with lace and velvet and silk, and don't be afraid to be a little experimental with your fashion choices. Whether you go for long, black manicured nails, fairy-like tie-dye or an edgy, grungy look, explore your wardrobe and find out what kind of clothes and accessories suit the witch you are inside.

As a side note, many witches like to keep a particular outfit for when they are doing spellwork and rituals. This would tradition-ally be a robe, but a luxurious silky dressing gown works just as well. It can add to the sense of occasion and ritual, and it can also be a great way to get yourself into that witchy headspace.

SELF-CONFIDENCE SPELL

A lot of the work we'll be doing on this journey will help to build your self-confidence, but for those times when you need a particular boost – perhaps because you're going to a big event that you're nervous about, or because you know you're going to see someone who makes you feel small – try this simple spell to channel a little badass energy, reminding you of how damn spectacular you are.

WHAT YOU'LL NEED

an orange candle
a small piece of rose quartz
a handful of rose petals
a cinnamon stick
an orange pouch or piece of cloth

WHEN TO DO IT

Do this whenever you need to, but you may find it particularly potent on a Tuesday, Thursday or Sunday thanks to their positive and affirming energies.

WHAT TO DO

Cast your circle (see page 42). In a calm and quiet frame of mind, light your candle and set it on your altar. Watch the flame for a few moments. Take the cinnamon stick and breathe in its spicy scent, then set it down on the altar. Next, inhale the delicious floral aroma of the rose petals, then scatter those across the altar too. Finally, take the rose quartz and clasp it between your hands. Gazing softly at the candle, summon the memory of a time when you felt confident and self-assured: perhaps delivering a speech that you knew you were well prepared for; perhaps when you were wearing a killer outfit that made you feel untouchable. Let those feelings of self-worth wash over you, and speak the following words:

Bold like spice and strong like stone
sweet like rose, let me be shown
the strength that lives within my core
self-doubt gone, of myself I'm sure.

Feel the energy radiating from within you. You are bold, strong and sweet. You can do whatever you put your mind to. You deserve to be where you want to be. You are allowed to take up space.

Sit with these feelings for a while longer, then place the rose quartz in the orange pouch (or wrap it in a piece of orange cloth), along with the rose petals and the cinnamon. Close the pouch and blow out the candle, then finish the spell and close the circle (see page 45).

Keep the pouch with you, in your pocket or in a bag, and whenever you need a little boost, take a moment to hold it and breathe in its scent.

Tarot for self-reflection

Practitioners have been using tarot cards for centuries, and many gifted seers are able to use them for divination purposes. If you've never had a full tarot reading, you should definitely try it; it's a completely unique experience and can be incredibly revealing.

Here, we're going to be looking at using tarot cards for self-reflection rather than true divination. This is about intuition, not prediction. A bad witch knows themself, and taking a few moments each day to sit with your tarot cards and reflect on what you've pulled can be really valuable. Plus, it feels witchy AF.

It's often said that your first tarot deck should be a gift from someone who loves you. If you're lucky enough to receive a tarot deck in this way, great. If not, you know who really loves you? YOU. Treat yourself to a beautiful deck. Buy it thoughtfully and imbue it with love, generosity and compassion for yourself.

For our purposes, we'll just look at a simple three-card reading, but if you find your work with the tarot resonates, there are many wonderful books out there that offer a deep dive into these beautiful and mysterious cards.

Take your tarot deck and shuffle it. If you have a particular question or concern that's troubling you, hold that in your mind as you shuffle. If you don't, that's fine; many tarot users just like to take a daily reading. Think of it as being a bit like checking a barometer.

When you feel ready, deal three cards, face up.

Look at the card in the middle first. This is your 'now' card. It reflects how things are for you in the present moment. Next, look at the card on the left. This is your 'past' card. It shows how things have been for you before. It might refer to the more distant past, or it might be something that happened last week. Finally, look at the card on the right. This is your 'future' card. It's not necessarily predicting what will happen in the future. It might just be inviting you to consider potential consequences, or showing you the way things might turn out if you continue on your current path. Take some time to consider all the cards together, musing on their meanings and thinking about the parts of your life they might relate to. Remember that the cards might not be talking about you, but about someone you know. For example, pulling the Magician in an inverted position might not mean that *you* are being prideful or manipulative, but that somebody is attempting to behave in that way towards you. Spending this time turning things over in your mind can really help you gain clarity around things that are bothering you.

I've given a very brief rundown of the cards' meanings below. You'll see that inverted (upside down) cards are usually thought to have different meanings to those that are dealt upright, but not all practitioners concern themselves with this. I have only included the Major Arcana, but most tarot decks also include the Minor Arcana, which is made up of four suits (Cups, Wands, Swords and Pentacles), each with a full set of number and court cards.

If you feel a connection to the tarot, I strongly suggest you seek out a more detailed guide. It's also worth bearing in mind that the tarot is open to interpretation. Some guides will have slightly different meanings for some cards. There's no need to get too hung up on this. The cards will tell you what they want you to know.

Main character energy

Number	Card	Upright	Inverted
0	The Fool	The start of a journey; potential for change; spontaneity	Recklessness and naivety; lacking energy or curiosity
1	The Magician	Power; wisdom; self-belief; new beginnings	Pride; manipulation; poor planning; lack of focus
2	The High Priestess	Intuition; spiritual growth; feminine power	Secrets and gossip; ignoring gut feelings
3	The Empress	Creativity; abundance; sensuality; fertility	Feeling uninspired or inadequate; creative block
4	The Emperor	Power; structure; father figure; authority	Controlling; arrogant; lack of order
5	The Hierophant	Stability; education; tradition; respect	Rigidity; conformity; focusing on social expectations rather than personal needs
6	The Lovers	Love; decision making; commitment; sexual desire	Uncertainty; inner conflict; low self-esteem
7	The Chariot	Diligence; willpower; personal strength; self-control	Unfocused; hindered by obstacles; feeling defeated
8	Strength	Inner strength; calm; courage; confidence; fortitude	Aggression; compulsive behaviour; self-doubt; in need of boundaries
9	The Hermit	Reflection; a need for solitude; searching for the truth	Withdrawal; disconnection; need for company and social support
10	The Wheel of Fortune	Luck; destiny; repetition of cycles	Bad luck; lack of control; a need to avoid risks
11	Justice	Fairness; taking responsibility; equality	Dishonesty; avoiding accountability; irrationality

12	The Hanged Man	Seeing things differently; reflection; patience; the need to make sacrifices; changing direction	Impatience; single-mindedness; stuck in one place
13	Death	Change; the end of something and the start of something new; letting go	Resistance to progress; a sign that something isn't over yet
14	Temperance	Purpose; self-control; compromise; moderation	Something is out of balance; excessive consumption or immoderate behaviour
15	The Devil	Desire; ambition; temptation	Addiction; obsession
16	The Tower	Sudden upheaval; crisis; the need to adapt	Fear of change; close call
17	The Star	Emerging from a hard time; rest and calm; optimism; inner peace; insight	Self-doubt, avoidant behaviour
18	The Moon	Hidden danger; a need to heed your intuition; illusion or artifice	Self-delusion; anxiety; a need to focus on logic rather than intuition
19	The Sun	Positivity; communication; strength and success; good health	Lack of joy; a need to allow more love in your life; feeling unimportant/insignificant
20	Judgement	Self-forgiveness; recognition of progress; reflection; atonement	Guilt; refusal to learn from mistakes; regret
21	The World	Fulfilment; freedom; travel	Stagnation; something is missing

Clear your space – and your mind

In order to keep the energy around you focused on what you really want, spend some time clearing your home of clutter and anything that has lingering negative energy. I'm not about to get all Marie Kondo on you, and I'm definitely not suggesting you get rid of *everything* – maximalism is witchy! – but if you have a gift from someone who you've since discovered is not worth your time, or perhaps an outfit that you can't help associating with the nastiness that happened the last time you wore it, clear that shit out. Essentially, get rid of things that are full of old, unwanted energy, and surround yourself with things you love. Don't feel guilty about getting rid of things that are holding you back. Curate your space.

Saturday is the perfect day to tackle this kind of task, as it's a day for cleansing and banishing negativity.

CLEANSING SPELL TO GET RID OF WHAT NO LONGER SERVES YOU

Even if you get rid of the physical items, sometimes bad feelings or energy linger around like guests who have long outstayed their welcome. Although you can't shove them into an Uber and call it a night, this cleansing spell is the next best thing. It can help you feel brand new and release the burden you've been shouldering.

WHAT YOU'LL NEED

a black candle
a bowl of water
salt
soil
a piece of paper and a pen

WHEN TO DO IT

Saturday is the perfect day for cleansing, and waning gibbous and the last quarter are both good moon phases for ridding yourself of toxic things.

WHAT TO DO

Cast your circle (see page 42) and light a black candle. Spend a few moments watching the flame and sitting with yourself. Take a large pinch of salt and sprinkle it into the water, followed by a large pinch of soil. Gently swirl the water around with your fingertips.

When you feel ready, take the pen and write down the thing you want to let go of. It might be a sense of bitterness towards someone who hurt you, but on whom you no longer wish to waste any more of your precious time or energy, or perhaps a feeling of not being enough that you really want to move past. I would suggest focusing on one thing at a time; if you write a whole list of things on your paper, your intentions could get muddled.

Carefully hold the corner of the paper to the candle's flame and allow it to catch light. Let the paper burn for a few moments (no need to hold on for too long; after all, this is about getting rid of things!), then blow out the flame and drop the paper into the bowl of water (don't panic if the flame doesn't go out when you blow on it; the water will sort it out!).

Now say:

With earth and air and fire and sea
I release the hold you have on me.
With sea and air and fire and earth
I move towards my own rebirth.

When you're ready, blow out the candle, close the circle and finish your spell (see page 45). Scoop the burned paper and any ashes out of the bowl and bury them outside in the earth.

CHAMOMILE AND ROSEMARY CLEANSING BATH

There is little I love more than a ritual bath. It's a decadent, delicious and relaxing way to witch. This cleansing bath is ideal for days when you have 'the ick' about everything and just want all that negativity to wash away.

WHAT YOU'LL NEED

a handful of your favourite bath salt
a handful of rosemary sprigs
a handful of dried chamomile flowers
a black candle

WHEN TO DO IT

Whenever you need it – but as we know, Saturday is a good cleansing day.

WHAT TO DO

Fill your bathtub with water at your preferred bathing temperature. Add the salt as the water is running, and swirl it around to dissolve. When you're ready to bathe, scatter the rosemary and chamomile over the water (or make a pouch – see page 32), then light your candle and immerse yourself in the soothing, cleansing water. Feel the bad energy and icky feelings gently wash away, and enjoy the sense of calm and control that remains.

PROTECTION SPELL

Main characters sometimes find themselves on the receiving end of less-than-pleasant behaviour from others. It happens to the best of us, and it can leave us feeling unsafe and insecure. Use this powerful protection spell if you feel under threat, and carry a sense of power and security with you.

This is a jar spell. Jar spells are simple and effective, and you can make them using different crystals, herbs and candles depending on your intention.

WHAT YOU'LL NEED

a white candle
a piece of paper and a pen
a small jar with a lid
a thyme sprig

a few black peppercorns
a few cloves
a crystal with protective properties, such as a
piece of jade, black tourmaline or turquoise

WHEN TO DO IT

Whenever you need to, but this may be particularly potent on a Tuesday, or if carried out during a waning gibbous moon phase.

WHAT TO DO

Cast your circle (see page 42) and light the candle. Take the paper and carefully write down what or who you seek protection from, and why. Try to state your reason clearly so that your intention is accurately set. Add the piece of paper to the jar, along with the thyme, pepper, cloves and crystal.

Close the jar, then carefully tilt the candle so that you can run the wax around the edge of the lid, sealing it. As you do so, say:

I seek protection from those who wish me harm
Keep me in a state of safety and calm.

When the jar is sealed, spend a few moments focusing on your intention, then blow out the candle, finish the spell and close the circle (see page 45).

If you wish, you can bury the jar in the earth somewhere close to your home (or even in a plant pot). If and when you no longer need its a protection, you can simply dig it up. If you prefer, you can carry the jar with you (although if you choose to do this, make sure you opt for a small enough jar).

Chapter 5:

IT'S NOT YOU, IT'S THEM – SPELLS FOR HANDLING ENERGY-DRAINING PEOPLE

We all have our own struggles, but some people just straight-up suck, whether it's the obnoxious mansplainer in your office who also manages to take credit for everyone else's work, the frenemy who always manages to get in a few jibes 'as a joke', or the toxic ex who keeps trying to worm their way back into your life (and your DMs).

Most of us have spent our lives being told to 'be nice'. We're faced with obnoxious or downright cruel behaviour, and we think the 'right' thing to do is smile and nod and let people stomp all over us.

Not any more. Maybe Mr Mansplainer needs to hold his tongue and stop claiming other people's ideas as his own. Maybe that toxic 'friend' needs to keep their distance. And maybe – just maybe

– it wouldn't be the worst thing in the world to (lightly) hex your ex.

You are on a spectacular path – we really don't want anyone getting in the way, do we?

CORD-CUTTING RITUAL TO END EMOTIONAL TIES

If you find yourself still emotionally or spiritually connected to someone who hurts you or makes you unhappy, this simple ritual can help to sever those energetic ties and free you from the painful connection. It's very straightforward but awash with symbolism, and the moment when the cord is severed can feel truly exhilarating.

WHAT YOU'LL NEED

two black candles
a metal tray or other fire-safe surface
a piece of string or thread

WHEN TO DO IT

This ritual may be particularly effective if practised on a Saturday, or during a waning gibbous or last quarter moon phase.

WHAT TO DO

This can be quite an emotional ritual, so take your time and be gentle with yourself. Arrange the candles a few inches apart on a metal tray or fire-safe surface. Carefully tie one end of the string around one candle, a short way down the candle's length, then tie the other end around the other candle (depending on how much time you have to devote to this, you might like to tie the string a bit further down to give you more meditation time, but it's up to you). As you tie the knots, think about the painful ties between you and the other person. Make sure the string is pulled taut between the candles.

When you're ready, light the candles. Sit comfortably in front of them and, as the flames glow, focus your energy on the connection being severed. Think about the sense of freedom and release you will feel when you are no longer bound to this person. Visualise the weight that will be lifted; imagine yourself dancing, free of the bonds that have held you down and made you feel so trapped. Continue to meditate on this until the candles have burned down to the string. When the flame reaches the string, it will ignite and burn, severing the tie. The string may drop and fall on the metal tray, or it might swing down to the side of one of the candles. Practise good candle safety and keep a close watch on it.

When the string is severed, you can blow out the candles. Gather any burned remains of the string and bury them in the earth a good distance away from your home.

Your bonds have been cut.

VARIATION

If the idea of waiting for the candles to burn down doesn't appeal, or if it all just feels a bit too fire hazard-y, you can simply stretch out a piece of string, meditate and visualise as above, and then, when the time feels right, cut it with a pair of scissors. Bury the cut pieces as above.

BINDING SPELL

If someone has caused you hurt or harm in the past, or is continuing to do so, or you suspect they may do the same to others, a binding spell can hamper or even put an end to their bad behaviour. It can be tempting to dive into dangerous hexes and very dark spells when someone has hurt us

– it's natural to want to hurt them back – but a binding spell allows you to flex your power and stop them in their tracks without putting you at the same kind of karmic risk. It's very much in keeping with the 'Do no harm, but take no shit' ethos we discussed earlier.

WHAT YOU'LL NEED

a piece of paper and a pen
a few cloves
a black ribbon or piece of cord

WHEN TO DO IT

This can be especially effective when carried out on a Tuesday or Saturday, or during a waning gibbous or last quarter moon phase.

WHAT TO DO

Cast your circle (see page 42) and light a black candle for protection. Sit calmly and quietly, and reflect on what you hope to achieve with this binding spell. When you're ready, write on the paper: 'I wish to bind [person's name] from', and then write down the particular behaviour. Try to be specific; you can't just say you wish to bind someone from being unkind, as it's too vague and nuanced an idea.

For example, you might write: *I wish to bind X from cruelly undermining my self-confidence and the self-confidence of other women he encounters.*

When you're happy with what you have written, place the cloves in the middle of the paper, then fold the paper around the cloves to enclose them. Next, slowly wrap the ribbon around the bundle. As you do so, say:

I safely bind [name] from their wicked ways.

Tie the ribbon in a knot, then blow out the candle, end the spell and close the circle (see page 45). Take the bundle to a place that's not too close to your home and bury it in the earth. Try to remember where you've buried it in case you ever need to come and dig it up. If you have any doubts as to whether you're doing the right thing for you, I'd advise caution. This is a powerful spell and shouldn't be carried out lightly.

SPELL TO GET THEM OUT OF YOUR HEAD

You know it's time to move on. You know ending the relationship/friendship/situationship was the right thing to do. You know they weren't making you happy or that they failed to appreciate you in all your glorious glory. Or maybe they treated you outright cruelly. And yet . . . you can't quite shake your feelings. You think about them more than you'd like. You find yourself idly scrolling to their Instagram to see what they're up to. You sometimes think about calling them when you've had a few too many. Even when you're trying to move past it and focus on you, they're still hanging over you in a cloud of confusing and painful feelings.

Sound familiar? We've all been there. But you know they're not good enough for a bad witch like you, so it's time to free up that headspace for what really matters. This spell can help release you from those lingering feelings that won't quite dissipate. And yes, it's essentially a witchy version of the Valentine's Day bonfire in Friends.

a black candle

a photo of the person (if you don't have a photo, you can write their name on a piece of paper instead)

a cauldron or fireproof bowl

black pepper

a handful of sage leaves

a small piece of haematite (optional)

a black cloth

WHEN TO DO IT

This may be particularly powerful if carried out on a Saturday or during a last quarter moon phase.

WHAT TO DO

Do this outside or in a very well-ventilated space.

Cast a circle (see page 42) and sit comfortably with all the items in front of you. Light the candle, then hold the photo (or piece of paper) and spend some time looking at it, thinking carefully about what you want to achieve with this spell.

When you're ready, hold the photo or paper up to the candle until it ignites, then carefully drop it into the cauldron. Add some black pepper and sage leaves for purifying and protection.* As you do so, say:

With flames and fire I am set free,
release the hold you have on me.
My mind, my heart, my soul are my own;
be gone from each, leave me alone.

When the fire has safely and completely burned out, transfer the contents of the cauldron into the middle of a piece of black cloth, then wrap it up into a bundle. If you like, you can add a small piece of haematite to the bundle to absorb any lingering bad energy. Blow out the candle, finish the spell and close the circle (see page 45), then take the bundle and bury it somewhere far from your home.

* Note: Please do **not** do a Rachel and add a splash of grappa. It will not end well.

FREEZING SPELL

As modern witches, we have access to many resources that weren't available to our witchy ancestors, but you may not have thought about kitchen appliances as being among them. Well, you were wrong. If there is someone in your life who just isn't getting the hint, this freezing spell can be a very literal way to 'freeze them out'. It's also a useful tool if you want to stop someone from gossiping about you – you can 'freeze' their tongue. As ever, be clear in your intentions and be aware that you shouldn't take action against others without carefully considering the consequences – if you, too, are prone to a little malicious gossip, your energy here could be misdirected.

WHAT YOU'LL NEED

a black candle
a piece of paper and a pen
a freezer-safe jar (or a zip-lock bag, but they
    don't feel quite so witchy)
water (extra points for moon water, see page
    40)
a few black peppercorns
a few cloves

WHEN TO DO IT

Give this spell a boost by doing it on a Saturday or during a last quarter moon phase.

WHAT TO DO

Cast a circle (see page 42) and light a black candle. Spend a few moments meditating on what you hope to achieve with this spell so that your intentions are clear. When you're ready, write the name of the person you want to 'freeze out' on the piece of paper. Then rotate the paper ninety degrees and write your intention on top of their name, so that your intention is on top of their name at a right angle.

Place the piece of paper in the jar, then pour in the water (taking care not to overfill the jar as the water will expand as it freezes). Add the peppercorns and cloves, then close the jar. As you do so, say:

Your word and actions hurt my peace,
with the power of ice, I bid you cease.

Blow out the candle, end the spell and close the circle (see page 45), then place the jar safely in your freezer. As the water freezes, the person's harmful behaviour will be frozen too.

If you wish, you can thaw it out when you're satisfied their negative influence has passed.

PROTECTION BRACELET SPELL

If you find yourself frequently faced with someone whose negative energy disrupts your day (perhaps a challenging colleague at work or a toxic person in your friendship group) but they are difficult to avoid, this protection bracelet can give you a boost and diminish their effect on you.

WHAT YOU'LL NEED

a black candle
a few drops of clove oil
a piece of black ribbon
three cloves

WHEN TO DO IT

This spell may be more effective if you carry it out on a Tuesday or Saturday, or during a waning gibbous moon phase.

WHAT TO DO

Cast a circle (see page 42) and dress the candle with a few drops of clove oil (see page 38). Wrap the ribbon around the base of the candle, then light the candle.

As you watch the flame, spend a few moments reflecting on what you hope to achieve, getting your intention clear in your mind.

After a few moments, as the candle burns, carefully remove the ribbon and hold it between your palms as if in prayer, thinking about how you want to feel – safe and protected. At this point, it's best to focus your energy on protection rather than the person you want to be protected from, or their negativity may interfere.

When you're satisfied that you have made your intentions clear, wrap the ribbon around your wrist and tie it securely. Blow out the candle, end the spell and close the circle (see page 45).

Wear the ribbon until it breaks. When it breaks, bury it in the earth with three cloves.

A SPELL TO REVEAL THEIR TRUE COLOURS

We've all had someone walk into our lives before who just seems, well, a bit off. And that's fine, it doesn't have to be a problem – except it is when everyone around you refuses to pick up on their negative, low-key hateful aura. Every time you hear 'they're just so lovely', you're fighting the very real urge to give them the bombastic, criminal side-eye and frankly it's draining. Instead of expending all your precious energy playing nice, it's time to get the person to reveal those true colours. Forget trying to catch them out with a three-way phone call à la Mean Girls *– it's not 2004 any more, sorry friends. Instead, this spell can help to clarify the truth and reveal someone as they truly are. Although small disclaimer: their 'true colours' may not be what you had expected. This spell isn't going to magically get everyone on side and oust someone from your circle, it's going to reveal the truth. And there is always a small but real chance that the person in question might actually be kind of nice once you get to know them . . . And, of course, if you're hiding something of your own, there could be some conflicting energies at play.*

WHAT YOU'LL NEED

a white candle
a photograph of the person (or a piece of paper
   with their name on it)
a handful of thyme leaves
a piece of white cloth

WHEN TO DO IT

This spell will work at any time, but you might choose a Monday (for intuition and knowledge), a Wednesday (for communication) or a waning gibbous or last quarter moon phase.

WHAT TO DO

Cast a circle (see page 42) and light the candle. Sit comfortably in front of it with the photo of the person (or the piece of paper). Take a few moments to set your intentions.

When you're ready, hold the photo or paper up to the candle's flame, but take care not to hold it too close: you don't want to burn or even singe it, you just want to shine a light on it. As you do so, say:

By the power of this candle's glow
let your truest colours show.

Focus your energy on making any illusions or fakery used by this person fail, and allowing others to see them as they truly are. When you're ready, place the photo in front of you and carefully hold the candle over it to pour a few drops of wax on to the image. Scatter the thyme leaves over the top; they should stick to the wax. Wrap it all up in a piece of white cloth.

Blow out the candle, end the spell and close the circle (see page 45), then bury the bundle in the earth.

A TASTE OF THEIR OWN BITTER MEDICINE

If there is someone in your life who seems to live for making the people around them feel as small as possible – I'm talking terrorising colleagues in the office just for fun kind of behaviour – this spell can help redirect some of their bitterness back to them. If someone insists on sending out such toxic energy, they really shouldn't be surprised if it comes back around twofold. Again, gentle disclaimer, this spell is designed to exact a little deserved justice so if you're equally guilty of bad behaviour or your anger is misdirected, it can end up backfiring . . . You wouldn't want the universe to send negative energy your way instead.

WHAT YOU'LL NEED

a black candle
a white candle

a piece of paper and a pen
a cup of vinegar
a pinch of salt
a few black peppercorns
a piece of black cloth

WHEN TO DO IT

Try this on a Tuesday or Saturday, or during a last quarter moon phase.

WHAT TO DO

Cast your circle (see page 42) and light the candles. Sit in quiet contemplation for a few moments, then begin to focus your energy on the person whose behaviour you'd like to see changed. Think about the way they behave and how it impacts other people. Write down their name on the paper, then drop it into the cup of vinegar. As you do so, say:

With salt and light and my best power,
let your cruel words taste truly sour.

Scatter over the salt and peppercorns, then spend a few moments imagining how the concoction in front of you would taste: sharp, bitter and biting.

Now imagine the person in question having their mouth flooded with that flavour every time they speak in a cruel or controlling way.

When you're ready, finish the spell and close the circle (see page 45). Take the cup outside and spread out the cloth on the ground, then pour the contents of the cup on to the cloth. Wrap up the paper and peppercorns in the vinegar-soaked cloth, then bury it in the earth.

Chapter 6:

ANOTHER DAY, ANOTHER DOLLAR – SPELLS FOR WORK AND MONEY

Work and money are two areas of life that can be incredibly stressful. We're surrounded by social media posts and podcasts promoting 'hustle culture', making us think that if we're not working all the hours Goddess sends and rapidly rising through the ranks, we're doing something wrong. Even when we do manage to get that dream job or longed-for promotion, many of us then find ourselves gripped by imposter syndrome, terrified that we're not good enough and that someone is going to 'find out'. Then there's the joy of navigating office politics, dealing with overbearing bosses and juggling deadlines at speeds that would dizzy the finest circus performer.

As for money – we're bad at talking about it, we hate admitting we need it, we never seem to have enough of it, and many of us are afraid that it's going to run out.

The 'solution' in both areas always seems to be to work *even* harder, to grind and hustle and grind some more, until we're on the brink of burnout and struggling to function.

Let's get real; that's not healthy and it's not sustainable – so let's look and see if we can find a few shortcuts here and there, a few tricks and twists to make the ride a little smoother. It's not selfish to want things to be easier, or to believe that you deserve better. It's OK to want the best for yourself because settling is not very bad-witch behaviour.

MONEY MAGNET SPELL

If your wallet is feeling a little skinny, try this money magnet spell to entice a little more cash into your life and fatten things up. Keep your focus on positivity, prosperity and abundance – always reaching for more, more, more. Go get that bag!

WHAT YOU'LL NEED

a green candle
a piece of green cloth
three coins
a pinch of fennel seeds
a few basil leaves
a whole nutmeg, or a pinch of ground nutmeg
a small piece of bloodstone or malachite
a piece of copper-coloured ribbon or wire
a basil plant (optional)

WHEN TO DO IT

Try this on a Thursday or during a waxing crescent moon to joyride on that extra prosperous energy.

WHAT TO DO

Cast a circle (page 42) and light your candle. Sit comfortably in front of it and take a few moments to think about what you want to achieve. Try to keep your energy positive and focused on abundance rather than dwelling on what is lacking. More attracts more.

Keep focusing on your intention as you place the three coins in the middle of the cloth, followed by the fennel seeds, basil leaves, nutmeg and blood-stone or malachite. Carefully wrap the cloth around these items. As you do so, say:

> *With coins and herbs I make my pact*
> *that greater riches I'll attract;*
> *with spice and stone I now invite*
> *wealth and gold and rich delight.*

Wrap the copper ribbon or wire around the bundle, then blow out the candle, finish the spell and close the circle (see page 45). Bury the bundle somewhere safe for seven days (if you have a basil plant, either in your garden or even in a pot, bury it in the soil beside the plant for extra potency).

SWEETEN THE DEAL JAR SPELL

Whether you're applying or interviewing for a new job, or hoping to get a promotion in your current workplace, this jar spell uses honey or sugar to sweeten others' opinions of you, and sesame seeds to open up new opportunities. Sesame seeds are a particular favourite of mine in this context: thanks to the phrase 'Open sesame!', which originally came from the story of 'Ali Baba and the Forty Thieves' in the Arabian Nights, *these powerful seeds are associated with opening up new path-ways and presenting new opportunities. They also taste amazing, so win-win.*

WHAT YOU'LL NEED

a green candle
a piece of paper and a pen
a half-finished jar of honey (or an empty glass
    jar and some honey or a few spoonfuls of
    sugar)
a pinch of sesame seeds
a cinnamon stick
a piece of fresh root ginger
a handful of rose petals
a small piece of citrine, granite and/or malachite

WHEN TO DO IT

You can do this any time, but it may be particu-larly successful if carried out on a Sunday or Tuesday, or during a waxing crescent or waxing gibbous moon phase.

WHAT TO DO

Cast a circle (see page 42) and light your candle. Sit for a few moments to set your attention and focus on what you want to achieve. When you're ready, write your intention on the paper, using language that suggests it *will* happen rather than you *hope* for it to happen. For example, you might write: 'I will be successful in my interview and will be offered the job.'

Keeping this intention clear in your mind, place the paper in the jar with the honey or sugar. Add the sesame seeds, focusing on the idea of doors opening. Add the cinnamon and ginger, focusing on success and abundance. Add the rose petals, focusing on luck. Lastly, add the stone or stones, focusing on victory, confidence and prosperity. As you do this, say:

With sweetness, spice and magic seed
let my wishes be achieved.

Put the lid on the jar and then, holding it carefully, drip the wax from the candle around the edge of the lid, sealing it.

End your spell (see page 45) and blow out the candle. Keep the jar somewhere safe: I recommend burying it in a flowerbed.

CONFIDENCE IS KEY RITUAL BATH

Have you ever been stunned by the confidence of that mediocre middle-aged man in your office? How is it that this deeply ordinary and beigely bland being feels able to speak up in meetings, while you find yourself holding back for fear of saying the wrong thing or looking like a loser? You know you're worth more than that.

This ritual bath allows you to soak in a confidence-building potion of petals and spice, with cinnamon for success, lavender for calmness and rose petals for self-esteem. Try it the night before an important work event, or if you're planning to ask your boss for a well-deserved pay rise. It doesn't have to relate to work and money, either; this can also help with social confidence and decision making. There is a deep core of awesomeness within you – let it come to the surface and shine.

WHAT YOU'LL NEED

a cinnamon stick
a handful of lavender
a handful of rose petals
an orange candle

a red candle
a small piece of granite

WHEN TO DO IT

Channel Tuesday's energy of strength and success, or try this during a first quarter or waxing gibbous moon phase.

WHAT TO DO

Fill your bathtub with warm water. When you're ready to get in, add the cinnamon to the tub, then scatter the lavender and rose petals over the water (or make a pouch – see page 32). Light your candles, place the piece of granite on the side of the tub and climb in, bathing in the boosting water and the warm glow of the candlelight. Focus your energy on your skills and achievements, and on how much else you still have to show the world. Keep your thoughts away from tedious little people and centre them on you. When you're done bathing, position the candles at either end of the bath and step out between them. Pick up the granite and carry it with you as a reminder of that powerful, confident energy. Then get out there and kick ass.

DANDELION CHARM FOR HYPNOTIC SPEECH

If you've got a pitch to make, a presentation to give or a big meeting where you need to dazzle, use this simple charm to boost your communication skills and make your words extra compelling.

WHAT YOU'LL NEED

a dandelion seedhead (a dandelion 'clock')
your own wicked breath

WHEN TO DO IT

Wednesday is the day for communication, or you could try this during a waxing crescent or first quarter moon phase.

WHAT TO DO

Simply pick the dandelion clock and stand facing east. Take a few moments to focus your intention. Imagine your tongue growing warm and visualise yourself speaking with precision, poise and eloquence. When you're ready, say:

*As these seeds drift on the breeze
to find new homes and grow,*

let my words take root and plant ideas
and let my talent and wonder show.

Take a deep breath and blow the dandelion seeds free, watching them drift away from you. Keep the stem in your pocket during the event or meeting as a reminder of how your words are going to spread.

BOUNDARY SPELL TO KEEP YOUR BOSS AT BAY

If you've got a boss who likes to email you late at night or call while you're on holiday, and doesn't seem to be able to grasp that some people might actually have a life outside the office, try using this boundary spell to draw a line. The spell can work both ways; it will deter your boss from keeping you on call 24/7, and it will also give you the resilience and confidence to say enough is enough, set some pretty clear boundaries and remember that you don't have to respond if you're not actually getting paid.

WHAT YOU'LL NEED

a black candle
an orange candle
a piece of paper and a pen or stick of charcoal
  (or, if you'd like to do this outside, a stick and
  a patch of earth)

WHEN TO DO IT

Tuesday's badass energies of protection and strength can boost your power here; this spell is also suited to waning crescent or new moon phases.

WHAT TO DO

If you want to do this outside, choose a place that feels like 'your' space, such as your garden. Cast your circle (see page 42) then light your candles. Sit comfortably and focus your intention on the person you want to set a boundary with, and what you want the boundary to be. For example, perhaps you want your boss to stop emailing you outside office hours, or maybe you want a colleague to stop texting you at the weekend. Keep their name or face in your mind so that your intentions are very clear and you don't inadvertently stop all your mates from calling you as well!

When you're ready, draw a line in the earth or on the paper, and say:

My walls are set and can't be breached,
my life's my own, I can't be reached.
Keep your energy at bay
at certain hours of the day.

When you're ready, blow out the candles, finish the spell and close the circle. If you used paper, bury it outside, somewhere near your home. If you drew your line in the earth, leave it there, and feel free to refresh it from time to time.

A CHARM TO LIE LOW

A beautiful witch like you is likely to always be turning heads, but all the attention can get kind of tiring and there are times when all of us just want to sort of . . . fade into the background. This can be particularly true at work – where flying under the radar can work hugely in your favour. For example, when your manager is looking to offload a particularly unappealing task on someone, or during one of those super enjoyable group meetings when you realise you're being asked to essentially take on a whole pile of extra work without any additional pay. This little charm means that people can still see you, but you won't be as noticeable. It will help their eyes just slide straight over you, and on to the unlucky colleagues sitting on either side. Just remember to remove the necklace when you do want to get noticed, or you could end up becoming just part of the furniture.

WHAT YOU'LL NEED

a black candle
a small piece of crystal that you feel represents
    you (spend some time looking at your crystals
    and choose the one that 'speaks' to you)
a length of copper wire
a length of ribbon or cord

WHEN TO DO IT

You can do this at any time, but the cleansing
energies of a Saturday or a waning gibbous or
last quarter moon phase could give it an extra
punch.

WHAT TO DO

Cast your circle (see page 42) and light the
candle. Spend a few moments sitting quietly,
focusing your intentions and getting yourself
ready.

Take the crystal and wrap the copper wire around
it in a 'cage' to hold the crystal, finishing with a
loop at the top. It doesn't have to look perfect.
Thread the ribbon or cord through the loop.

When the candle has burned down enough to give you plenty of wax, carefully lift the candle and drip the wax on to the crystal. It might take a few attempts; the idea is to coat the crystal as well as you can. As you do this, say:

Although I'm here, I'm barely seen
concealed behind a waxen screen.

When the crystal is coated, let the wax harden and dry. Blow out the candle, finish the spell and close the circle (see page 45). Keep the wax-coated crystal necklace somewhere safe, and put it on when you want to go barely noticed. This is most potent in small doses. If you decide to wear it all day, every day, it can become less effective – or things could go the other way, and you could find people start forgetting about you in a way that doesn't feel good. If you don't like the look or feel of the wax (especially if it's a hot day and things feel a little melty), you can pop the amulet in a little pouch and wear that around your neck instead.

STRESS-BANISHING RITUAL

If you've had one of those weeks where the to-do list just keeps growing and you've felt your stress levels on the up and up, this ritual will help you reset and refocus on what really matters – you. With lavender to calm you and a hint of black pepper to keep the negativity away, this is a great ritual to do at the weekend when you want all things work-related to get in the bin.

WHAT YOU'LL NEED

a blue candle
a blanket
a bunch of lavender sprigs
freshly ground black pepper
a piece of amethyst

WHEN TO DO IT

The ideal time for this is on a Saturday, or during a last quarter moon or waning crescent moon phase.

WHAT TO DO

Light the candle, then spread out your blanket on the floor. Arrange the lavender sprigs around the edges of the blanket, forming a sort of border or frame. Scatter black pepper over the lavender. Lie down on the blanket, safely encircled by the flowers. Lie on your back with your eyes closed. Hold the amethyst between your hands, just over your heart.

Allow your breathing to become slow and steady as you imagine the lavender 'wall' pushing all your stresses away. Let the amethyst's calming energy flow down into your heart and trickle through your veins. Close yourself to stress and anxiety.

Stay here for as long as you need to, then blow out the candle. Carry the amethyst with you as a reminder of this soothing ritual.

Chapter 7:

WAKE UP AND CHOOSE CHAOS – SPELLS FOR GENERAL MISCHIEF

If you can't help but indulge in a little *Schadenfreude* when something goes wrong for someone with whom you fundamentally disagree, this could be the chapter for you. We've already established that we don't want to actively harm anyone, but if people are already circulating negative energy, why not just . . . help things along a bit?

UK readers may remember a particularly disastrous speech given by ex-prime minister Theresa May at the 2017 Conservative party conference. As she spoke, she kept coughing as if there was a persistent bug in her throat, and by the end she almost couldn't get her words out. Someone had to rush to her aid with a throat sweet. Watching the footage of that event (especially when the sign behind her started falling down), I couldn't help imagining a gleeful left-wing witch out there, someone who didn't want to actually harm the PM, but who wanted to interrupt her speech and cause a little chaos.

From the feminist group WITCH (Women's International Terrorist Conspiracy from Hell) hexing Wall Street in 1968 to present-day witches casting curses at Donald Trump, using magic to protest, disrupt and generally sow mischief can be a wonderful way to embrace your darker side.

These spells can be practised alone or with some pals as part of a coven (see page 46). If you opt for the latter, I suggest you make a day of it, mix up a few Bloody Marys and wholeheartedly embrace the chaos.

SPELL TO RAIN ON THEIR PARADE

Even the most dedicated of bigots doesn't like to get wet, so this simple rain spell is a great way to disrupt an event you disagree with. Perhaps a certain misogynist politician is holding an outdoor rally; maybe a narrow-minded hate group are planning a march. Of course, showing up to visibly and safely counter-protest is important here, but getting the weather on your side can really help to put a dampener on their event. As with any weather spell, be clear in your intentions and keep calm as you cast, to make sure you don't induce a dangerous downpour.

WHAT YOU'LL NEED

a black candle
a map showing the location of the event
a pen
a handful of dried rice or grain

WHEN TO DO IT

As close to the event in question as possible.

WHAT TO DO

Alone or with your coven, cast your circle (see page 42) and light the candle. Spend a few moments focusing your intention. Think about the event you want to disrupt, but take care to avoid focusing on your anger or frustration with the person or group in question. Weather spells can be unpredictable, so it's important to avoid imbuing this with too much negativity. The people you're trying to disrupt have enough negativity for all of us.

When you're ready, draw a circle on the map around the place where the event is due to be held, and then write the name or a description of the event within the circle, so that your intent is crystal clear. Now hold your handful of rice or grain over the map and slowly start to sprinkle the grains down on to it. If you're working in a group, take a few grains each and take turns to sprinkle them. As you do this, think of rain, but again keep your mind on soggy feet and messed-up hair, not flash floods or other dangerous outcomes. At the same time, say:

I call the rain to quell your crowds
to damp your fires with heavy clouds;
with drizzle, downpour and constant shower
I quench the hate that gives you power.

When you're ready, fold up the map in a bundle with the rice or grain inside. Blow out the candle, then end the spell and close the circle (see page 45). Keep the bundle somewhere safe until the event has passed – and don't be surprised if you get a little wet, too.

BINDING SPELL TO CHALLENGE A PUBLIC FIGURE

This is similar to the binding spell used on page 78, but instead of being directed at someone you know personally, it's for use against a public figure – perhaps a politician or high-profile figure whose behaviour or values you consider harmful. This can be done alone or in a group. As with any binding spell, keep your intentions clear and focused.

WHAT YOU'LL NEED

a black candle
a candle in a colour that you feel represents how
   the person uses their influence for harm (see
   colours on page 37) – for example, if it's
   someone who uses their wealth to gain power
   and harm others, choose a green candle
a small piece of haematite
a long piece of black cord
a piece of black cloth

WHEN TO DO IT

This spell may be particularly effective if done on a Saturday or during a waning gibbous or last quarter moon phase.

WHAT TO DO

Alone or with your coven, cast a circle (see page 42) and light both candles. Take a few moments to focus very clearly on the person you're targeting and the way in which you want to bind them. When you're ready, lift the coloured candle and allow a few drops of the wax to fall on to the haematite. Then blow out the candle and begin to wind the cord around it, all along its length. If you're in a group, take turns doing this until the candle is completely bound. As you do so, speak your intention clearly. For example, you might say:

[Name], I bind you from using your wealth and influence to harm vulnerable people.

When you are finished, wrap the coloured candle and the haematite in the cloth. Blow out the black candle, then end the spell and close the circle (see page 45). Bury the bundle in the earth somewhere not too near your home, but at a location you'll remember if you ever need to retrieve it.

REFLECTION JAR SPELL TO RETURN NEGATIVE ENERGY TO THE SENDER

If there is someone (or a group of someones) throwing harmful, hateful, negative energy out into the world, there's no need to waste your own energy on trying to stop them. Use this simple mirror spell to bounce that energy back towards them, then sit back with a glass of red and watch with glee as their vile systems crumble. This is the sort of spell that could see a hypocrite caught out by breaking one of their own rules, or a person who spreads lies being revealed as a dangerous manipulator. As ever, be aware that your own slate might not be squeaky clean, and be prepared for the potential consequences.

WHAT YOU'LL NEED

a black candle
a jar with a lid
a sheet of tin foil
an item to represent the person or group, such
    as a political pamphlet, a photo cut out from a
    newspaper, or a button or badge
a handful of salt

WHEN TO DO IT

This could work especially well on a Saturday or Tuesday, or during a waning gibbous or last quarter moon phase.

WHAT TO DO

Alone or with your coven, cast a circle (see page 42). Light the candle, then spend a few moments focusing your intentions on what you want to achieve. Carefully line the inside of the jar with the foil, making sure the shiniest side is facing inwards. Add the item representing the person or group to the jar. As you do so, say:

> *The greatest hate out there's your own*
> *so let its power chill your bones.*
> *With mirror work I cast it back*
> *so it can stop you in your tracks.*

If there's a group of you, you can chant this together. Sprinkle the salt into the jar, visualising a mirror reflecting the person or group's angry faces back at them. Close the jar and use the black candle to seal the lid with wax. When you're ready, blow out the candle, then end the spell and close the circle. Bury the jar in the earth somewhere not too close to your home, but in a place where you can return and retrieve it if you need to.

Undoing a spell

As I explained earlier, it's important to think carefully about your intentions and potential consequences when casting a spell. The universe is a complicated and chaotic place, and magic doesn't always behave in the ways we expect it to. If you realise you have cast a spell that you shouldn't have, and find yourself feeling regretful, then you can try this undoing spell in an effort to reverse it. It requires you to make a sacrifice of something meaningful to you, so it can't be done lightly. You can't just merrily cast whatever spell you want and then scribble it out if you change your mind. Karma has a long memory.

WHAT YOU'LL NEED

as many white candles as you can reasonably lay
   your hands on
rosemary oil
any items you still have from the spell you
   want to undo (for example, if you made a jar

spell or buried a bundle and you're able to access it)

a piece of paper and a pen

a piece of black cloth and some string

a few sage leaves

a few rosemary sprigs

a few thyme sprigs

a handful of salt

a handful of black peppercorns

an item that has meaning to you, such as a piece of jewellery, a beloved knick-knack or a favourite book – just don't use a photo, as you may end up sacrificing the thing *in* the photo instead of the photo itself

WHEN TO DO IT

Make use of the cleansing energy of a Saturday or a waning gibbous moon phase.

WHAT TO DO

Anoint the candles with rosemary oil and let the oil dry. Cast your circle (see page 42) and light the candles. If you have any items from the spell, lay them in front of you. Spend a few moments reflecting on the spell you wish to undo. Be real with yourself about why you cast it, and why you now regret that. Write down the details of the spell: the date you cast it, why you did it, and what you attempted to do. Rotate the paper and write over the top of this, at a right angle: 'I take back this spell.'

Lay out the black cloth in front of you and place any items from the spell on it. (If it was a jar spell, break the seal and tip out the contents.) Place the piece of paper on the cloth too, along with the sage, rosemary and thyme. Sprinkle over the salt and pepper. As you do this, say:

On [date], I cast a spell
please break its hold and make all well.

Focus your energy on dismantling the spell. Remember how it felt to cast it and try to imagine reversing that sensation.

Take the item that you have chosen to sacrifice and place it on top of the bundle. Say:

I sacrifice this [name of object] to the universe in payment.

When you're ready, wrap up the bundle and tie it tightly with the string. Blow out the candles, finish the spell and close the circle (see page 45). Bury the bundle in the earth.

I would suggest taking a cleansing bath with plenty of salt (and more white candles) to remove any lingering negative energy.

PART THREE:

LIVE DELICIOUSLY – SELF-CARE INSPIRED BY THE SEVEN DEADLY SINS

'There's a little witch in all of us.'
– Alice Hoffman, *Practical Magic*

The Seven Deadly Sins

We've looked at basic witchery, we've explored how to use spellwork and rituals to make things go your way (and cause a little chaos), but now it's time for a deep dive into sin – and how it can be an incredibly empowering and effective form of self-care.

I'm sure we've all seen those 'That Girl' videos on social media, where an astonishingly awake young woman leaps out of bed at 5 a.m. with what looks suspiciously like a full face of make-up, dons her designer yoga pants, does downward dog for all of five seconds, writes in a gratitude journal, makes a matcha latte with a machine that cost more than my flat, carries out an elaborate skin-care routine that involves more bottles than a well-stocked liquor cabinet, then eats half a rice cracker and two almonds while sitting at her immaculate desk. #morningroutine #selfcare

I mean, you do you, love, but the kind of self-care I'm talking about doesn't involve denial, virtuousness or stretching. I see your half a rice cake, and I raise you a bowlful of tiramisu. Now that's a breakfast I can get involved with.

Although they don't actually feature in the Bible, the Seven Deadly Sins are considered a Christian construct and are closely associated with the religion. They come with a hefty dose of judgement, shame and self-flagellation. They are:

Gluttony (overindulgence)
Lust (giving in to carnal desire)
Greed/avarice (desire of material possessions)
Sloth (laziness)
Wrath (rage and fury)
Envy (jealousy and wanting what others have)
Pride (selfishness and self-pleasure)

Now, call me crazy, but I don't think any of those things sound deadly. I think they sound human, natural – and *fun*.

We're here for a good time, not a long time. Let's do this.

Chapter 8:

GLUTTONY

I think gluttony or greed is a concept with which many of us have difficult and shameful associations. We have ideas of 'good' foods and 'bad' foods; we live in a society that judges different body types and eating habits, often cruelly. We grew up around magazines and media that celebrated and lauded self-denial, dieting and shrinking into nothing. When we go out for a meal with friends and the waiter asks, 'Would you like dessert?' we often look at each other, waiting to see who will say 'yes' first, none of us wanting to be the person who does. We watched our mothers and aunts and role models drink grainy meal-replacement shakes or eat limp salads; we learned to be wary around things that were creamy, rich and sweet.

It's time to reject these feelings of shame around food and indulgence, and instead embrace the visceral, bodily pleasure of consumption. Take those feelings of eating being 'bad' and flip them around – because we *like* being bad. It's fucking delicious.

With every crunch, bite, nibble and lick, celebrating food, flavour and fullness is a subversive, witchy and challenging act.

FEASTING RITUAL

This ritual is designed to help you embrace indulgence and enjoy food without any sense of shame or guilt. It can be a valuable ritual for boosting self-worth, as often we don't allow ourselves things we'll enjoy because we feel on some level that we don't deserve them. You, my witchy pal, deserve whatever you desire. You can carry out this ritual with friends, and it's honestly a joyful experience to share, but I'd recommend doing it alone at least once, because there's something deeply affecting about it. If you're a culinary witch, you can of course choose to do this with home-cooked food, but I've suggested getting food delivered to really focus on the indulgence. Choose whatever you fancy; order from more than one place. Order more than you need. Leftovers are always delicious. Reject diet culture, reject judgement, reject calorie-counting and obsession. It is time to feast.

Gluttony

WHAT YOU'LL NEED

a picnic blanket
green, orange and blue candles
atmospheric music
your favourite wine or other beverage
plates
takeaway food

WHEN TO DO IT

You can do this whenever the mood strikes, but
Fridays and Sundays suit this ritual particularly
well, as does the abundant energy of the full moon
phase.

WHAT TO DO

Prepare your space before the food arrives. Lay
the picnic blanket on the floor, and light the
candles. Choose some sensual, atmospheric music,
then pour yourself a generous drink.

When the food arrives, arrange it invitingly on
the blanket, laying it out on pretty plates.
Position the food in a circle with you in the
middle. Sit surrounded by these delectable treats;
inhale the delicious aromas. Take a deep swig of

your drink, then reach out and begin to eat. Bonus points if you eat with your hands. Relish each mouthful; notice the textures and flavours, and the way they combine. Let sauce run down your chin; don't worry about table manners. Indulge, enjoy, ingest.

When you're full, lie back on the blanket and revel in the delicious glory of a sumptuous feast.

SPICED SALT SPELL FOR CULINARY WITCHES

Everyone knows salt makes everything taste better, but this salt adds another dimension. If you're a keen cook, use it to give your dishes a magical flavour boost.

WHAT YOU'LL NEED

a green candle
a frying pan
1 teaspoon cumin seeds
a pestle and mortar
4 tablespoons flaky sea salt
a pinch of dried chilli flakes
freshly ground black pepper
a small jar

WHEN TO DO IT

This spell will work at any time, but channelling the good-luck energy of a Thursday or a first quarter moon phase could help your food turn out even more deliciously.

WHAT TO DO

Cast a circle (see page 42) around yourself and your hob (because it will be difficult to cast a salt or elemental circle in this case, I'd suggest an energy circle where pesky things like walls won't get in the way). Light the candle, then place the frying pan over a medium heat and lightly toast the cumin seeds for about half a minute until the kitchen fills with their fragrance. Tip them into the pestle and mortar, then grind them lightly. Now combine them in a bowl with the salt, chilli flakes and pepper. Stir together, saying:

Salt and spice to enhance flavour,
make every meal a delight to savour.

When you're finished, transfer to the jar, then blow out the candle, finish the spell and close the circle (see page 45). Sprinkle your delicious, spiced salt on anything savoury and delight in the flavour-enhancing properties.

CHOCOLATE MEDITATION RITUAL

Whether your preference is for wickedly dark chocolate or an outrageously creamy white, this chocolate meditation ritual helps you reconnect with the sheer sumptuous delight of eating.

WHAT YOU'LL NEED

a comfortable place to lie down
orange and red candles
a piece of your favourite chocolate

WHEN TO DO IT

Do this whenever you need a hit of indulgent deliciousness, but it feels especially suited to the seductive energy of a Friday.

WHAT TO DO

Light the candles and lie down in your chosen place. Try to ensure you're surrounded by material comforts: soft pillows, warm blankets, silky throws. When you're ready, take a piece of chocolate and place it on your tongue. Lie back, close your eyes, and allow the chocolate to melt. Eat it slowly, luxuriating in the sensuality of this sweet and delicious food. As you do so, remind yourself that you are deeply deserving of this joyful, decadent experience.

VARIATION

If chocolate isn't your bag, you can do this with any kind of food. The idea is just to focus on one mouthful at a time and really luxuriate in the experience.

WITCHY WAYS TO EMBRACE GLUTTONY

✳ Don't pay attention to what anyone else is ordering; just choose whatever calls to you.

✳ Enjoy an ice cream at night or when it's raining. It hits differently.

✳ Satisfy each of your senses at every meal. Mix textures, breathe in aromas, and enjoy creating elaborate and beautiful platefuls.

✳ Being a bad witch takes energy. Never deny yourself something you're craving.

Chapter 9:

LUST

Our culture has a very strange attitude towards lust and sex. We tend to value physical beauty above all else, celebrating bodies that fit into certain narrow parameters, but if the owners of said bodies seem to be enjoying them a little too much, society is very quick to condemn them. We're all familiar with the idea of someone being 'slut-shamed', and all too often the attitudes are deeply gendered, with men celebrated and women derided for doing exactly the same thing.

Whatever your gender identity, a good bad witch knows that enjoying their body, truly connecting with it and inhabiting it, is the key to exploring earthly delights. In this chapter, we'll be looking at spells and rituals to help us move away from feelings of shame around sex and lust, and instead embrace them with horny enthusiasm.

So stop dimming the lights (unless that's your thing), embrace your kinks, and let's get freaky.

SENSUAL SELF-MASSAGE SPELL

We've talked about body image before, and sadly it's an issue that can stop many of us from fully enjoying sex. This spell is a saucy little self-massage to help you unlock your inner sex god(dess) and boost your confidence in the boudoir.

WHAT YOU'LL NEED

a comfortable, safe space
pink and red candles
rose petals
massage oil (something with rose, jasmine and/
    or ylang-ylang would be ideal)
your sexy naked (or partially clothed) self

WHEN TO DO IT

Fridays are all about sexy energy, or you could try this during a waxing gibbous or full moon phase.

WHAT TO DO

Set up your space in a way that feels comfortable and safe to you: perhaps you'll pile blankets and pillows on the floor, put on some music to set the mood – whatever feels right.

Cast your circle (see page 42) and light the candles. Scatter the rose petals in a ring around you, then sit or lie down. Pour some of the massage oil into your hands and slowly start to massage yourself. Start with your arms, then your legs, moving down to your feet, then work your way back up to your torso. Use long, slow, sensuous strokes, taking your time to notice how it feels and how delicious the oil smells. As you do this, say:

*I worship my body with oil and light
to fill it with love on this special night.
With roses and candles and sensual touch
my body deserves to be worshipped this much.*

Let the massage go on for as long as feels good to you (and if other things happen, they happen). When you're ready, blow out the candles, end the spell and close the circle. Try to keep that slow, sensual, dark feminine energy with you as you go.

SWEET APPLE SPELL TO ATTRACT A LOVER

If self-massage isn't quite hitting the spot, and you're really keen for a particular person to join you, channel your lust into this attraction spell. Apples, rose oil and a little candle carving make this a delightful little bit of spellwork, but it comes with a caveat: we heart consent. That means the spell will only work if the person you're trying to attract wants it to. You can't change their mind or turn them into a mindless love zombie (haven't you seen The Craft?). *What you can do is send out a wave of sexy energy that'll have them sliding into your DMs on the double – as long as they want to.*

WHAT YOU'LL NEED

a red candle
rose essential oil
a pin
an apple
a knife

WHEN TO DO IT

Try this on a Friday to enhance its seductive energy, or during a first quarter moon phase.

WHAT TO DO

Cast your circle (see page 42). Dress the candle with rose essential oil (see page 38), then carve the name of the person you hope to attract into the wax. Light the candle, then slowly peel the apple with the knife. If you're able to keep the peel in one long, sexy spiral, then great, but this isn't essential. As you peel the apple, murmur the name of the person.

When you're done, arrange the apple peel around the base of the candle and say:

[Name], with this candle red
I invite you warmly to my bed.
If it's your will, then come to me
and we'll be joined in ecstasy.

Now eat the apple in slow, juicy bites, enjoying the sweet tanginess. When you're finished, blow out the candle, end the spell and close the circle (see page 45), then bury the apple core and peel, and the candle, in the earth.

SEXY BATHING RITUAL

If you have a lover coming to visit, or perhaps if you're just looking forward to some one-on-one time with a favourite toy, this bathing ritual is an indulgent way to get you warmed up and ready to rock and roll. With lavender to get you feeling relaxed and loved up, rose petals for romance and a vanilla pod for sensual energy, this is a veritable love potion – and you're about to jump right in.

WHAT YOU'LL NEED

a handful of bathing salt
a few lavender sprigs
a handful of rose petals
a vanilla pod
red and pink candles

WHAT TO DO

Fill your bathtub with delightfully warm water at your preferred bathing temperature. Add the salt as the water is running, and swirl it around to dissolve. When you're ready to bathe, scatter the lavender, rose petals and vanilla over the water (or make a pouch – see page 32), then light your candles and climb in. Let the floral, fragrant water lap at your skin and fill you with desire. Focus your thoughts on your favourite sexy memories or sensual experiences, and feel your body wake up and come alive with passion.

WITCHY WAYS TO EMBRACE LUST

- Make a list of your sexual fantasies – no matter how outlandish – and things that you'd like to try in the future.
- Don't be shy about saying what you want. If the other person shames you or reacts unkindly, they don't get to enjoy your gorgeous body. (If they're respectful, but just not into what you've suggested, show them the same respect in turn and don't push it.)
- Dance naked (in the comfort of your own home) when the mood takes you. It's liberating, thrilling and helps you connect with your body.
- If you usually do it with the lights off, turn them on. Sometimes a change-up can be an incredible turn-on. On the other hand, if you're usually a lights-on kinda witch, experiment with having a sexy sesh in

total darkness – are any of your other senses heightened?

✳ Wear sexy underwear on an ordinary day.

✳ Don't wear any underwear at all.

Chapter 10:

GREED/AVARICE

'Don't be greedy.'

It's a common enough refrain from our child-hoods, whether our parents were scolding us for taking the largest piece of cake, not wanting to share our toys or taking a longer go on a favourite piece of playground equipment.

Don't be greedy.

Let someone else take a turn.

Let this little boy go first.

OK, but – hear me out – why? Why is it wrong to want what we want? And why are we taught that the 'right' thing to do is to let someone else have it instead?

Fine, everyone remembers that one little prick from school who never let anyone else have a go on the best climbing frame, and he *was* annoying, but maybe he also kind of had a point.

Greed is often tangled up with feelings of shame and we can find ourselves in a vicious cycle of self-admonishment, so this chapter is about letting go of the conditioning that we are somehow less entitled to the things we want than other people. It's about shaking off the feelings of discomfort and embarrassment we have about saying what we want – and taking it.

Whether it's food, money, material goods, little treats, big treats – whatever it is, you deserve *more*.

It's your turn.

A RITUAL TO WELCOME ABUNDANCE

This ritual is an important first step towards welcoming abundance into your life. Because that's all greed is, really: wanting the things you want. And wanting more of them. By focusing your energy and mindset on abundance and plenty, you move away from a place of lack and emptiness, and towards one of attraction and manifestation.

WHAT YOU'LL NEED

a green candle
an orange candle
a neutral oil, like sunflower oil
fennel seeds
dried rose petals

WHEN TO DO IT

Embrace Thursday's prosperous energy, or try this during a waxing crescent, first quarter, waxing gibbous or full moon phase, when energy is focused towards attraction.

WHAT TO DO

Take your candles and rub a little oil along their lengths, then roll them in the fennel seeds and rose petals. They should stick to the oil, but don't worry too much if some fall off. Light the candles, sit comfortably, and begin to focus your energy on the idea of *more*.

You might picture a library packed with fascinating books, a cupboard stacked with delicious foods, a wardrobe filled with beautiful clothes – it's up to you. One of my favourite things to visualise is a tower of glasses, with champagne bubbling up and out of each one. Make an effort to keep your energy positive here – if you find yourself veering towards negative thoughts about what you don't have, steer yourself back to visualising more, more, *more*. When you're ready, blow out the candles and try to hold on to that sense of being ready to receive the gifts of the universe.

STRING SPELL

Don't be fooled by the apparent simplicity of this spell. String magic can be potent, and a lot of concentration is required to get your desired outcome. Be specific, be focused, and get what you came for.

WHAT YOU'LL NEED

a piece of ribbon or string

WHEN TO DO IT

This spell takes place over several nights during a waxing moon phase (a waxing moon phase usually lasts about seven nights, so plan accordingly).

WHAT TO DO

On the first night of a waxing moon phase, sit down somewhere comfortable while holding your string. If you are able to do this somewhere the moonlight shines on you, even better.

Focus your attention carefully on what you want. Try to be specific: don't just say, 'I want more money,' because there are a lot of ways that could happen, and not all of them are good (plus, two pence more than what you currently have is technically 'more money'). Name what you want and how you'd like it to happen. With your mind focused on this, tie a knot in the end of the string furthest from you.

The next night, do the same thing, tying another knot, this one a bit closer towards you. Repeat this each night for the rest of the moon phase. Keep the string somewhere safe.

PROSPERITY SPELL

Whether you're after a significant financial boost or just hoping to receive some truly spectacular gifts for your birthday, this spell helps you attract good luck and material abundance. Creating a charm to carry around with you means that the magnetic attraction energy is always present, so whenever the opportunity arises, you are ready to receive.

A note: this is unlikely to take effect if you just perform the spell and take no further action. You need to take steps that will enable the abundance to reach you, whether that's applying for a new job, requesting a pay review or even making an online wish list featuring the things you really want. You're just clearing a path so the magic knows where to flow.

WHAT YOU'LL NEED

a green candle
an orange candle
a cinnamon stick
a piece of citrine
a piece of agate

a small green pouch
a piece of copper-coloured ribbon or wire

A waxing crescent moon phase is the perfect time for this spell. If you can do it on a Thursday too, even better.

Cast your circle (see page 42) and light the candles. Sit comfortably and focus your intention clearly on what you want to attract. When you're ready, drip a little of the candle wax from each candle on to the cinnamon stick. When it dries, place the cinnamon stick in the pouch, along with the citrine and the agate. Take the copper ribbon or wire and wrap it three times around the neck of the pouch, then tie it shut. As you do so, say:

With jewels and spice, I do invite
an abundance of riches and delight.
This magic pouch will help them find me
I leave my days of want behind me.

When you're ready, blow out the candles, end the spell and close the circle. Carry the pouch with you wherever you go to attract the things you want.

WITCHY WAYS TO EMBRACE
GREED/AVARICE

✴ More attracts more. Lean in to maximalism and fill your space with things that delight you, from fresh flowers and gorgeous plants to stunning artwork and sumptuous soft furnishings.

✴ When you're in attraction mode, try to adopt open body language. Avoid crossing your arms and legs, as this pushes energy away from you.

✴ If someone offers you something you want, don't say, 'Are you sure?' or 'If you really don't mind.' Smile and say, 'Yes, please.'

✴ Treat yourself to little things on a daily basis to help you get used to the idea of deserving the things you want. Grab a coffee on the way to work from your favourite place, buy yourself flowers, pick up a new candle or spell book. You're worth it.

Chapter 11:

SLOTH

They say the devil makes work for idle hands, but that's a risk I'm willing to take. If we're constantly on the go, achieving this, ticking that off the to-do list, and planning and scheduling our lives down to the minute, when do we get a chance to stop and breathe and, you know, have fun? People like to talk about how we should work hard and play hard – I'd like to add 'rest hard' to that list.

We live in a world obsessed with hustle culture, impressed by the grind, where CEOs of tech start-ups tell us that they 'made it happen' by getting up at 4 a.m. every day (and conveniently fail to mention they have incredibly rich parents). We're exhausted, burned out, running on empty and increasingly bitter. We're ashamed of rest, and we've forgotten how to do it.

As a witch who is proud to rebel against societal norms, you should embrace the sin of Sloth whole-heartedly. As well as recharging your energy for your next round of mischief, you'll be channelling the wisdom of the Crone (see page 22), who symbolises repose.

So wrap yourself up in a duvet, turn on your 'out of office' reply, and hang up a sign on the door that says, 'Gone witchin'.' It's time to enter goblin mode.

TURN YOUR TO-DO LIST TO ASH

This simple ritual utilises the cleansing energy of fire to help you feel less pressured by obligations and outstanding tasks. Unfortunately, it won't make the obligations and tasks go away entirely (I'm still working on that spell . . .), but it will help you gain a sense of perspective on what's really important, and help you to reset and reposition yourself so that you can put your own needs first instead of those of others.

WHAT YOU'LL NEED

a blue candle
a black candle

a piece of paper and a pen
a cauldron or fireproof container
a handful of sage leaves

WHEN TO DO IT

Do this when you're feeling overwhelmed and under pressure. The cleansing energy of the waning gibbous moon or a Saturday may feel particularly appropriate.

WHAT TO DO

Do this outside or in a very well-ventilated space.

Light your candles, then sit down with your pen and paper and write out a list of all the pressing tasks and to-dos that are crowding your mind. They can be small ('sort out that online return') or big ('get my career sorted'). They don't have to be in any particular order. Just let them all pour out of you. This part of the ritual can feel stressful because the list is a visual reminder of why you've been feeling under pressure, but just take your time.

When you're done, spend a few minutes breathing calmly and focusing on the candles. When you're ready, hold the paper up to the flame until it catches, then drop it into the cauldron to burn. Add the sage leaves to the fire and let their cleansing smoke release you from the pressures of the list.

As the list burns, watch your words disappear and enjoy the feeling of the responsibilities and stress turning to smoke and ash. When the fire has safely burned out, let it cool, then bury the ashes in the earth.

SAFE HOUSE SPELL

Many witches use charms and spellwork to protect their homes. This spell is a spin on this idea, with a focus not just on protecting your home from harm, but also from general disturbance. It's a bit like putting your space on 'do not disturb' mode. It won't make you unreachable, so if there's an emergency, the people who need to get to you still can. It'll just create a slight barrier, a gentle resistance, that will leave potential botherers inclined to leave you in peace.

Sloth

a black candle
a blue candle
a pestle and mortar
a small handful of black peppercorns
dried chamomile flowers
a few dried lavender sprigs
a small handful of dried thyme
a black pouch
a small piece of amethyst
a small piece of rose quartz

WHEN TO DO IT

Do this whenever you need a real duvet day. The waning gibbous moon phase is a particularly good time.

WHAT TO DO

Cast your circle (see page 42) and light the candles. Place the pestle and mortar in front of you and spend a few moments focusing your intentions on what you want: a day of rest and quiet, when the little annoyances of daily life will fall away and nobody will bother you with trivia or drama.

When you're ready, add the peppercorns, chamomile, lavender and thyme to the mortar and begin to grind them together with the pestle. As you do this, say:

Of petty troubles let me be released
so I may have a day of peace.

When the mixture is ground into a powder, tip it into the pouch and add the amethyst and rose quartz. Close the pouch and hold it. Visualise someone walking up to your door, then hesitating and deciding to come another day; or perhaps picture your boss typing out an email, and then deciding to chat to you about it on Monday instead. When you're ready, blow out the candles, finish the spell and close the circle (see page 45). Take a small pinch of the powder from the pouch and sprinkle it in front of the door (or doors, if you have more than one) to your home. Then hang the pouch over your door.

When you're ready to rejoin the world, remove the pouch and sweep up any sprinkled herbs.

REST-DAY RITUAL BATH

There is nothing more indulgent and glorious than taking a bath in the middle of the day, just because you feel like it. It is the ultimate slothful, hustle-rejecting, self-focused move – so what are you waiting for? With chamomile for peace and calm and lavender for rest, you'll be floating away on a cloud of chill in no time. You can, of course, enjoy this ritual bath in the evening if you prefer, but for me there's something deliciously subversive about taking yourself off to bathe in the afternoon.

WHAT YOU'LL NEED

white, brown and blue candles
a handful of bath salts
a handful of lavender sprigs
a handful of chamomile flowers
a piece of haematite
a piece of amethyst
a glass of wine or a cup of chamomile tea

WHEN TO DO IT

Whenever you wish. The waning crescent moon phase is a time to rest and recharge, and Saturdays are good for cleansing and self-care.

WHAT TO DO

Light the candles and fill a bath with warm water. As the bath is running, add the bath salts and swirl them around to help them dissolve. When you're ready to bathe, scatter the lavender and chamomile over the water. Place the haematite at the door to absorb negativity, then place the amethyst by the side of the bath. Disrobe and climb in, then reach for your wine or tea and lie back amid the steaming, fragrant water, sipping your drink and doing . . . Absolutely. Nothing.

WITCHY WAYS TO EMBRACE SLOTH

✳ Treat yourself to some outrageously comfortable loungewear: something soft, ideally fleecy and definitely cosy.

✳ Get comfortable with saying 'no' to things you don't want to do. Do you really want to go and queue up for two hours to try and get into that wanky new bar that doesn't take reservations? No, you want to stay at home eating ramen and watching a true-crime documentary. *So do it.*

✳ Discover the joy of the afternoon nap. Taking a little snooze when the 2 p.m. slump hits isn't the exclusive reserve of snotty toddlers and the elderly. Treating yourself to some mid-afternoon shuteye can help boost your energy for the rest of the day, perfect for when you've got some late-night rituals planned.

✳ Build yourself a witchy nest out of duvets, blankets and pillows, gather all your favourite treats, and have a movie marathon: *Hocus Pocus*, *Beetlejuice* and *The Craft* are all essentials here.

Chapter 12:

WRATH

Wrath, anger, fury, rage – whatever you call it, there's no denying it's a powerful emotion. It's also one that we're encouraged not to indulge in. How often in life do we swallow down feelings of anger and frustration, and instead smile politely and nod along, trying not to rock the boat? We're taught to comply, to behave, to *be nice*.

But here's the thing. It's OK to be angry. In fact, there's a lot to be angry about. The world is full of hateful, bigoted people who have a lot of power and use it in vile ways. Of course you're pissed off.

Because anger is such a powerful feeling, it's important to learn to channel it correctly. If you're not careful, and just continue smiling and nodding and *being nice*, that anger can fester inside you. It can even turn inwards. Think about how uncomfortable that hot ball of rage feels when someone wrongs you. Do you really want that to stay inside your body? Better to express it, release its awesome power and use it.

Being nice is overrated.

RAGE RITUAL: BREAK STUFF

Sometimes it can be hard to find a target for our anger. It might be because we're enraged by a situation rather than a particular person or action, or it might be because, despite our fury, we're not really up for dancing the old rule of three tango by throwing a negative spell in the direction of the person we're pissed off with. This ritual is about embracing and expressing anger that feels like it has nowhere to go, instead of trying to swallow it down.

WHAT YOU'LL NEED

a black candle
a red candle
an old china plate that you no longer need
a permanent marker
a dustpan and brush
a piece of black cloth
a small piece of haematite

WHEN TO DO IT

This really is a ritual to carry out when the need hits. Anger is not an emotion that waits around for a convenient moon phase.

WHAT TO DO

Make sure you're wearing shoes.

Light your candles and sit with the plate in front of you. Spend a few moments sitting with your anger. This can feel quite alien; we're so used to trying to push these feelings down. It can be liberating and a little alarming to let them rush over you instead. Pay attention to how the fury feels: is it bubbling up inside you, or swooshing through your veins?

When you're ready, write some words on the plate that express how you're feeling, for example 'frustrated', 'challenged', 'powerless', 'humiliated'. Note that we're not writing the name of the person or people, nor are we writing about the cause of your anger.

When you're ready, stand on a hard surface (somewhere it's safe to do this), hold the plate up and smash it to the ground, letting it shatter into pieces. Feel the rage burst out as you do so.

Allow yourself a few moments to appreciate the power of the moment, then carefully sweep up the fragments and place them on the black cloth, taking care of the sharp edges. Place a piece of haematite in the pile too, to absorb negativity, then carefully wrap the cloth around the fragments and bury the bundle in the earth.

PRIMAL SCREAM RITUAL

This ritual is particularly useful for working through feelings of shame we often hold around anger. We think we should have more 'self-control' and not let things get to us so much. But we're human, and part of being human is getting royally fucked off every now and again. Instead of trying to pretend you don't care or that 'it's no big deal', channel your fury into a powerful scream and own it.

A word to the wise: this ritual needs to be carried out somewhere you won't alarm people nearby with your unearthly howling. If you live with others, warn them in advance, or find somewhere remote or relatively soundproofed. A lot of people like to do this in their cars, but make sure you're being safe if you go for this option. Personally, I find letting it all out at a super loud gig is the best way forward – you can scream along with the music and unleash all that power into a room that's already vibrating with energy.

WHAT YOU'LL NEED

your voice
an appropriate space

WHEN TO DO IT

Again, whenever you need to – as long as you don't scare the living shit out of your neighbours.

WHAT TO DO

Let the anger flow through you. As before, notice how it feels in your body, how it bubbles and fizzes and boils. Allow your rage to grow. Then, focus your energy on the *power* of the rage – not how it festers and hardens when kept inside, but the intense potential energy you feel when you consider unleashing it.

Now, throw back your head and scream. Wholeheartedly, whole-throatedly, roar your rage into the air, stepping into your own self as a formidable witch who isn't afraid to express their feelings.

Feel better?

ANGER INFUSION SPELL

This is a spell for when you want to turn your anger into energy with the hope of using that energy for something else in the future. By infusing a piece of absorbent haematite with your rage, you can 'bottle' it and use the power at a later date. I recommend adding a piece of turquoise or emerald to the jar to help cleanse any negativity, keeping the potency of the power without imbuing it with negative feelings that could play havoc with your future spellwork.

Wrath

a black candle
a piece of haematite
a glass jar with a lid
a piece of turquoise or emerald
a handful of sage
a white candle

WHEN TO DO IT

Wrath calls when she calls, but if you're dealing with the lingering type, a waning gibbous moon phase is the perfect time to let go.

WHAT TO DO

Cast your circle (see page 42) and light the black candle. Sit in quiet meditation, holding the haematite and focusing on your feelings of rage. Again, pay attention to how the anger feels in your body and really let it wash over you, safe in the security of your circle. With both hands clasping the haematite, imagine your fury flowing through you and into the porous, absorbent stone. If your rage seems to have a colour – for many of us, it's red – imagine the stone glowing with that colour as the anger pours into it.

As you do this, say:

> *Into this rock I pour my rage*
> *and bind it safe with stone and sage.*
> *Hold my fury safe for me*
> *and turn it into energy.*

Put the haematite into the jar and quickly add the turquoise or emerald and sage, then pop on the lid. Carefully tilt the black candle and pour some of the wax around the top of the jar to seal it. Blow out the black candle and light the white candle. Spend a few moments sitting in its calming glow, allowing a sense of peace and wellbeing to flow over you. When you're ready, add some of the white wax to the jar's seal as well. Blow out the candle, finish your spell and close the circle (see page 45). Bury the jar in the earth, somewhere you can find it again – and no one else will.

WITCHY WAYS TO EMBRACE WRATH

✳ Get comfortable with naming your anger. If someone pisses you off, it's OK to tell them. It doesn't mean you have to be a dick about it (unless they deserve it, of course).

✳ If you have somewhere you can safely light a fire, then do so. Put some music on, invite over some coven mates (or do it alone if you prefer) and dance it all out.

✳ If you're musically inclined, turn your rage into a song. Some of the greatest music out there had its birth in anger.

✳ Use the power of your rage to propel you forward. It's a cliché, but it's true: the best revenge is a life well lived.

Chapter 13:

ENVY

Envy is a tricky one. For the purposes of this book, we'll be considering envy to mean wanting something that someone else has, or feeling bitter because they have it. Envy can often manifest itself in wishing bad things on the person you're envious of, or taking a cruel pleasure in their misfortunes when things do go wrong. And hey, there's nothing wrong with a bit of *Schadenfreude*; when someone has genuinely behaved like a shit-bag, it's natural to feel gleeful when they get their comeuppance. But there's no need to let things get too ugly – that's a lot of energy to waste on someone you don't even like.

Envy doesn't have to be malicious. It can motiv-ate you, by helping you identify exactly what it is that you want. And if you spend some time under-standing how envy works, you can begin to see how it affects other people too, which can be deeply powerful knowledge.

As with the other Seven Deadly Sins, we've been taught that envy is an emotion to be ashamed of. We hate to admit to feeling it, and we cringe when we criticise someone or something only for a friend who knows us a little too well to piously intone, 'You're just jealous.'

But there's a liberating power in honesty, and owning our feelings (even the ones we wish we didn't have) can be deeply freeing. Bad witches don't hold back.

You know, green eyes look good on you . . .

GREEN-EYED MONSTER MEDITATION

This ritual meditation encourages you to sit down with your green-eyed monster and truly listen to what they're trying to tell you. Do you really hate Alison from marketing because she's smug AF, or do you actually envy her because she has something you want? And when you look at it a little more closely, is there any reason why you shouldn't have the thing, too? How did she get it? How can you get it? Use your envy to your own advantage, to crystallise your goals and get things in motion.

WHAT YOU'LL NEED

a white candle
a violet candle
a piece of emerald or turquoise
a piece of rose quartz
a piece of paper and a pen

WHEN TO DO IT

This is a useful meditation to turn to whenever envy takes you over, but if you've really been stewing on something, use the clean start of a new moon phase or the intuitive energy of a Monday to do a deep dive.

WHAT TO DO

Light the candles and sit or lie comfortably somewhere quiet where you won't be disturbed. Clasp the piece of emerald or turquoise in your left hand and the rose quartz in your right.

Take a few breaths, then, when you're ready, turn your attention to the object of your envy. Begin by indulging in a little good old-fashioned jealousy. Allow yourself to feel bitter and frustrated if that's how you feel. Pay attention to how the envy feels in your body – imagine it moving through you. What colour is it? We always associate envy with green, but what shade? An acid chartreuse or a deep, sludgy khaki? A bold apple green or a rich, foresty tone? Imagine this energy flowing into the green stone.

Consider the object of your envy again, this time allowing yourself to look at them from a more objective viewpoint. Imagine you're a disinterested third-party observer. What is it that this person has that makes you envious?

If you're envious of the person because you fancy their partner, this isn't about focusing on wanting that specific partner for yourself. It's about identifying what it is about the relationship that appeals to you, and working out how that might look for you. Likewise, if the person has a job that makes you seethe with emerald longing, don't focus on that particular job – they already have it. Identify what it is about the job that appeals to you. Is it the pay packet, the career progression, the way their boss treats them, the swanky offices? Get really clear on this and try to drill down into it until you can really understand a few key points that are the true focus of your desire. For example, *I want a partner with a wicked sense of humour but who knows when to be serious,* or *I want to have a clear idea of where my career is going; I'm sick of feeling a bit lost and unsure of myself.*

Once you're clear on this, then turn your attention to the piece of rose quartz and let its self-esteem-boosting glow flow into you. Whatever it is you have identified, you deserve it.

When you're ready, write down what you want on the paper. Keep it somewhere safe with the stones while you work on what you're after.

If you like, you can try the string spell on page 144 or the money magnet spell on page 94 to help you move towards achieving your true desire.

A word to the wise: if this meditation actually serves to crystallise that Alison is in fact an unbearable and toxic person, peruse the spells in Chapter 5 and see if you can find another way to get her out of your precious headspace.

ENVY REVELATION SPELL

This spell is designed to help you use the envy of others to your best advantage. If you have a suspicion that someone is sending negative energy your way because they're envious of what you have, perform this spell to reveal their feelings. Knowing what makes them jealous has two key effects: one, you can use this knowledge to your own advantage when navigating interactions with them – nothing wrong with a gentle flex here and there if someone's causing you trouble – and two, it can give you a wicked boost of self-confidence – 'Why yes, my fashion sense is absolutely killer, thank you for bloody noticing.'

Once you understand someone's envy, you can protect yourself from any hateful vibes they're sending your way, and get a clearer idea of how to handle them.

WHAT YOU'LL NEED

a white candle
a black candle
a bowl of water
a pinch of ground nutmeg
a few thyme leaves
a small piece of jade
a piece of white cloth

Envy

This spell will work at any time, but the waning gibbous moon phase is a great time to embrace knowledge and practise self-protection.

WHAT TO DO

Cast your circle (see page 42) and light the candles. Look down into the bowl of water. If you can see your reflection in it, great. If not, just visualise it. Imagine you're not looking at your reflection, but seeing yourself as the other person sees you.

When you're ready, scatter the nutmeg and thyme leaves over the surface of the water, then carefully lift the candles over the bowl and drip some of the black and white wax into the water. It should harden as it hits the surface. As you do so, say:

With water, wax and wonder
let your envy be revealed.
Show me how you see me
and what has been concealed.

Imagine the surface of the water shimmering and clearing as a new, true 'reflection' appears. The truth probably won't be revealed to you just yet; you simply need to focus on the idea of *knowing*. When you're ready, scoop the pieces of hardened wax out of the water and wrap them and the jade in a piece of white cloth. Blow out the candles, finish the spell and close the circle (see page 45). Keep the bundle somewhere safe until the understanding of the person's envy comes to you.

When you have the knowledge you need, use it wisely.

JAR SPELL TO TAKE THE STING OUT OF ENVY

We've established that envy can be a good thing, in that it can motivate you and help you achieve what you really want, and I hope that by now you're clear that it's definitely nothing to be ashamed of. Envy is a natural human emotion and we all experience it at times. However, it can be a tricky feeling to handle. It's kind of spiky and it can sting you when you least expect it. If you're finding it all too bitter and want to take the edge off, this spell uses honey and haematite to bind the sting while leaving you with that all-important self-knowledge.

WHAT YOU'LL NEED

a black candle
a pin
a small plate
a piece of cotton wool, or something similarly
    soft
a glass jar with a lid
a small piece of haematite
a thyme sprig
a spoonful of honey

WHEN TO DO IT

The cleansing energy of a Saturday can give this spell an extra kick, or you could try it during a waning gibbous or last quarter moon phase. Allow yourself a little extra time with this spell, as we're letting the candle burn right down.

WHAT TO DO

Cast your circle (see page 42) and light the candle. Place the pin on the plate and spend a few moments looking at it, focusing your thoughts on the unpleasant prick of bitterness that you feel when envy overtakes you. When you have that clear in your mind, pick up the candle and let a few drops of wax fall on to the pointy end of the pin, then set the candle back down. When the wax has hardened, wrap the pin in the cotton wool, imagining you are cushioning its wicked sting. Place this in the jar, followed by the haematite and thyme. Drizzle over the honey, and imagine its sweetness countering the bitter taste of your jealousy. Now close the jar and drip some candle wax around its edges to seal. Drip a blob of wax on to the lid of the jar and use it to secure the candle on top of the jar. Once this is done, say:

Blunted by wax, softened with wool
my envy's sting is not so cruel.
Take away its bitter bite
with honey, thyme and haematite.

Now let the candle burn down. Its wax should spread and pool over the jar, keeping that spiky sting well encased. Blow out the candle, close your circle and finish the spell, then bury the jar somewhere in the earth.

WITCHY WAYS TO EMBRACE ENVY

✷ Name it. There's nothing to be ashamed of here, as I think I've made abundantly clear, and speaking your envy aloud ensures it doesn't have a hold over you. Tell the person, 'Wow, I'm so jealous of your job/family life/ability to stay awake during meetings.' You'll give them a little boost – always fun to spread that good energy around – and they might even share their secret or tell you that it's not all as glossy as it first appeared.

✷ Use the strong feelings envy invokes in you in your spellwork – just take care not to send out any energy that you can't handle.

✷ Get comfortable with seeing envy as a way to reach out for what you want. Envy doesn't control you, it works for you – use it.

Chapter 14:

PRIDE

As I'm sure has been made unquestionably clear by now, we are firmly pro sin in this book, but of all the delicious, subversive treats offered by our beloved Seven Deadlies, Pride has to be the tastiest. It's also the one that makes least sense as a sin. It really just comes down to accepting your own innate awesomeness. What in the world is wrong with that?

Too often, we're taught to downplay our achievements or talents. We're made to feel there is something inherently bad about enjoying success or talking about the things we're good at. If someone tells you they love your outfit, do you grin and say, 'Yeah, me too,' or do you blush and say, 'Oh, it was actually on sale,' or something self-denigrating?

Imagine dropping this commitment to always appearing humble and self-effacing, and instead stepping boldly into your own self – full of confidence, full of energy, full of pride.

Because damn – you're good.

EPIC SELF-LOVE RITUAL BATH

This ritual bath is essentially an exercise in soaking up your own awesomeness. It's about giving yourself all the things you deserve, and allowing the warm, glowing feeling of self-love to penetrate every element of your being. This ritual can be used as a celebration of self when you're already feeling as proud as you deserve to be, but it can also be used to kickstart those gorgeous feelings if you find yourself at a low point and in need of a self-esteem boost. Inspired by legends of Cleopatra indulging in milk baths, I've included an optional milky addition to take the decadence to dizzying new levels.

WHAT YOU'LL NEED

orange and pink candles (as many as you can)
a handful of bath salts
a cup of blended oats or coconut milk powder
    (optional)

a handful of rose petals
a piece of rose quartz

WHEN TO DO IT

You can do this whenever you need a boost, but Sunday's joyous energy or the intoxicating power of the full moon can make it even more potent.

WHAT TO DO

Run a bath full of hot, steamy water. As the water is running, add the bath salts and the blended oats or coconut milk (if using) and swirl them around to disperse. Light the candles and position them around the tub, filling the room with a gorgeous glow. Scatter the petals across the water (or use a pouch – see page 32) and place the rose quartz on the side of the tub.

Climb in and sink into the fragrant water. As you lie back let yourself delight, unashamedly, in your own excellence: your strong, beautiful body; your bold, brilliant mind; your wild, wonderful powers; your unmatchable creativity; your quick wit and darkly delicious humour.

Think about each of the things you love about yourself. Take the piece of rose quartz and hold it under the water as you think about these things, focusing on them, enjoying them, and feeling that amazing energy drift around you.

After your bath, keep the rose quartz with you as a reminder of your brilliance.

WINE RITUAL TO CELEBRATE SUCCESS

This ritual is for those moments in your life when you have had a success and you want to mark it. It helps you take the time to celebrate yourself, and also cements the moment in your memory, ensuring you never forget how excellent you are. Think of this as raising a glass to yourself. I've suggested using red wine because it is both indulgent and delicious, but if you want to switch up the drink, feel free.

WHAT YOU'LL NEED

a green candle
an orange candle
a mirror
a glass of red wine
a cinnamon stick

a few cloves
a few saffron strands (optional)

WHEN TO DO IT

You can do this whenever you have something worth celebrating. The positive growth energy of the waxing gibbous moon may feel particularly appropriate to you.

WHAT TO DO

Light the candles and sit or stand in front of a mirror. Take your glass of red wine (or other drink) and drop in the cinnamon stick and cloves to infuse it with abundant positive energy. If you have saffron, sprinkle over a few strands to signify this special moment. Lift the glass to your nose and inhale deeply: note the spicy fragrance of the cinnamon and cloves mingling with the richness of the wine. Look at yourself in the mirror and congratulate yourself on your achievement. If you want to, you can say it out loud. It can be as simple as, *I did it.*

When you're ready and full of pride, raise the glass to your reflection, and drink deeply (but not so deeply that you swallow a mouthful of spices).

I did it.

Hold that sense of achievement and success with you, and return to it whenever you need a reminder of how brilliant you are.

PRIDE-BOOSTING JAR SPELL

You have a lot to be proud of. You're a gloriously bad witch with a wealth of talents, after all. But sometimes even the best of us can run a little low on self-esteem. This pride-boosting spell helps you remember how amazing you are, and if you make it in a small jar, you can carry it with you whenever you need a hit of self-love. Because you know who gets shit done? Witches who believe they can.

WHAT YOU'LL NEED

a violet candle
a pink candle
an orange candle
a small jar with a lid
a pinch of ground ginger
a pinch of ground nutmeg

a few rose petals
a small piece of marble or serpentine
a small piece of rose quartz

WHEN TO DO IT

Monday, Tuesday or Sunday would be excellent days to make this spell jar – or try it during a full moon phase.

WHAT TO DO

Cast a circle (see page 42) and light your candles: violet to give you the wisdom to see your own excellence, pink to enhance your sense of self-love and compassion, and orange to boost your mood and leave you feeling strong and happy.

Arrange the candles in a spaced-out triangle on your altar, and place the jar in the middle. Focus your feelings on congratulating and celebrating yourself. Think about the qualities you have that you'd like to be prouder of, and imagine yourself flooded with positive, powerful energy. When you're ready, add the ginger, nutmeg and rose petals to the jar, followed by the marble or serpentine and rose quartz. As you do this, say:

On this day and at this hour
I am reminded of my power,
my strength, my wisdom and my skill
to help me do all that I will.

Close the jar and drip some of the wax from each candle around the edge of the lid to seal it. Let the wax dry, then blow out the candles, finish the spell and close the circle (see page 45). Keep the jar with you for a powerful boost.

WITCHY WAYS TO EMBRACE PRIDE

✳ If you've done something you're proud of, tell the world about it. Whether you ran a marathon, smashed a deadline, made the most amazing cake in the world or just look really fucking good in that new dress, take a picture and share it with the world. Own your successes and shout about them.

✳ Get comfortable with acknowledging and celebrating the things you're good at. Start small if you need to; if saying, 'I'm an amazing cook' feels too challenging at first, start by saying, 'I made a next-level penne alla vodka last night.'

✳ Whenever you achieve or recognise something you're proud of, reward yourself in a tangible way. It doesn't have to be a huge reward, but it should feel significant and relevant. A witchy friend of mine has a charm bracelet where each charm represents an achievement she is proud of. For my part, I like to get a new tattoo to celebrate particular successes and keep them current in my mind.

Conclusion:

THE BEST KIND OF BAD

None of us is inherently good or bad. We're all made of a delicious concoction of a little bit of both. We all have days when we feel angelic, and days when we feel positively devilish. I hope that with this book, I've shown you that leaning into that 'bad' side, allowing a bit of the darkness in, can actually be a lot healthier (and a hell of a lot more fun) than trying to squash it down and deny it. It can't always be rainbows and butterflies; sometimes it has to be storm clouds and wasps, and that's OK. As long as you're not trying to swallow the storms and wasps down and keep them inside you. That's just a recipe for disaster – and not the fun kind.

There is a kind of badness that is malicious, that seeks to actively harm innocent people and destroy things out of cruelty. But the badness we've explored together here is not like that. It's not really 'bad' at all. It's just honesty. It's just boldness. It's just resisting and pushing back against the things that make us feel shit, and hungrily embracing the things that make us feel amazing.

There's a dark, giddy kind of joy to it, isn't there?

'Selfish' isn't a dirty word, it's an excellent one. If you're being selfish, you're honouring yourself and all the witches who came before you by refusing to take anyone else's shit and prioritising your own delight.

So go on – take what you deserve. Have a second helping. Pour yourself a glass of wine on a Tuesday. Run a hot, bubbling bath in the middle of the day. Post that selfie where you look fucking glorious. Turn off your phone when your boss calls you. Light the candles, cast a circle and practise the spells and rituals that will bring you all the things you desire, and keep away the things that are just too tedious for words.

Life is short, you're unstoppable, and damn, you look good in black.

Blessed be.

About the Author

Lily Hart lives in a cottage in the woods with her black cat, Lucifer. She's on a mission to reclaim black magic for bad witches everywhere – because well-behaved witches never made history. That said, all her enemies have perished in mysterious circumstances.